SOUTHAMPTON FOOTBALL CLUB
ANNUAL 2018

SOUTHAMPTON FC

DRAPER Tools DRAPER Tools DRAPER Tools DRAPER Tools

Written by Gordon Simpson and Tom Biggs
Designed by The 16K Design Works

A Grange Publication

ISBN: 978-1-911287-80-3

CONTENTS

5 WELCOME
6 SEASON REVIEW
17 TOP IMAGES OF THE SEASON
18 EFL CUP FINAL
20 PLAYER AWARDS
22 QUIZ OF THE SEASON
24 TOP FIVE GOALS
25 TOP FIVE GAMES
26 TOP FIVE ASSISTS
27 MANOLO'S MAGIC MONTH
29 SAINTS PUZZLES
30 MEET THE NEW BOYS
33 MEET THE NEW BOSS
34 TEAMMATES WITH CHARLIE AUSTIN
36 NEW KIT
38 PLAYER PROFILES
48 SPOT THE DIFFERENCE
50 GOALKEEPING TIPS WITH VINCE BARTRAM
52 KIT ROOM SECRETS
54 STRENGTHEN YOUR GAME
56 PREMIER LEAGUE FOCUS
60 QUIZ ANSWERS
62 SPOT THE SAINTS

WELCOME TO THE

SOUTHAMPTON FOOTBALL CLUB ANNUAL 2018!

OVER THE NEXT 60 PAGES, WE'RE BRINGING YOU A HOST OF FANTASTIC FEATURES FOR FANS OF THE CLUB TO ENJOY – WHATEVER YOUR AGE!

We start with a look back at what was a positive 2016/17 season as the club once again secured a top-eight finish in the Premier League and memorably reached the EFL Cup final at Wembley Stadium.

We also take a special look back at that day against Manchester United, as our supporters took over the famous ground and helped the players produce an inspired performance that deserved so much more.

Additionally, we introduce you to Saints' new manager, Mauricio Pellegrino, and all of the club's summer signings, meaning you will be well set ahead of the 2017/18 campaign.

As if that wasn't enough, we've also got our big quiz of the year, as well as a host of other puzzles, to test your knowledge.

On top of all that, we bring you some great features from behind-the-scenes at Staplewood to give you a few tips on your game and an insight into what happens at the training ground.

Enjoy your read!

SEASON REVIEW

A NEW MANAGER, NEW EUROPEAN ADVENTURES AND A MEMORABLE RUN TO THE EFL CUP FINAL.

Southampton's 2016/17 campaign was not short of drama, as they aimed to continue their incredible progression of recent years.

Saints' season will be remembered for their fantastic 2-1 win against Italian giants Internazionale in the UEFA Europa League, their semi-final success against Liverpool in the EFL Cup, and their fourth consecutive top-eight finish in the Premier League.

Despite the result, no Saints fan will ever forget the club's first major final since 2003, following a stunning run in the EFL Cup, in which they saw off four Premier League sides without conceding a goal, before falling to Manchester United in the final.

Here, we relive all the highs and lows of another positive campaign for Saints...

AUGUST

A sixth-place finish in 2015/16 meant Saints didn't have to worry about any Europa League qualifiers this time around, so Claude Puel's first game in charge came at home to Watford in the Premier League. Nathan Redmond's debut goal salvaged a well-deserved point for Saints, who had fallen behind to a strike from Etienne Capoue.

There would be no third successive league win at Old Trafford, as Saints' first away game of the season ended in a 2-0 loss to Manchester United. **Zlatan Ibrahimović** scored both goals for **José Mourinho**'s side.

Sunderland were up next for Saints and, despite dominating, they fell behind when **Jermain Defoe** scored from the penalty spot. But, just as they had done against Watford, **Puel**'s men fought back well and earned a point thanks to **Jay Rodriguez**'s powerful finish.

The month would end with Saints completing the signing of attacking playmaker **Sofiane Boufal**, who joined for a club-record fee from Lille, much to the excitement of the club's supporters.

SEASON

SEPTEMBER

A new month brought fresh hope for Saints as they headed to Emirates Stadium to face Arsenal. Puel's men put in a spirited performance, and went ahead through Petr Cech's own-goal, but lost out to Laurent Koscielny's volley and a last-gasp penalty from Santi Cazorla.

A first win of the season soon arrived on a memorable night at St Mary's in the UEFA Europa League. **Charlie Austin** scored twice and **Jay Rodriguez** grabbed a third in a terrific 3-0 win against Sparta Praha.

With confidence renewed, Saints grabbed their first league win of the season three days later, as **Austin** scored the only goal of the game in a 1-0 victory against Swansea City.

And when **Austin** opened the scoring against Crystal Palace in the EFL Cup in Saints' next game, few would have predicted the incredible run **Puel**'s men were set to enjoy in the competition. Academy graduate **Jake Hesketh** added the second, with his first professional goal, in a 2-0 win against the Eagles.

Three wins in a row soon became four, along with another clean sheet, as Saints swept aside West Ham United at London Stadium. **Charlie Austin** continued his fine form with the opener, before **Dušan Tadić** added a second. **James Ward-Prowse**'s first league goal from open play sealed a fantastic 3-0 win.

The month ended with a respectable 0-0 draw in Israel against **Hapoel Be'er Sheva**, as **Puel**'s men made it four points from their opening two European fixtures.

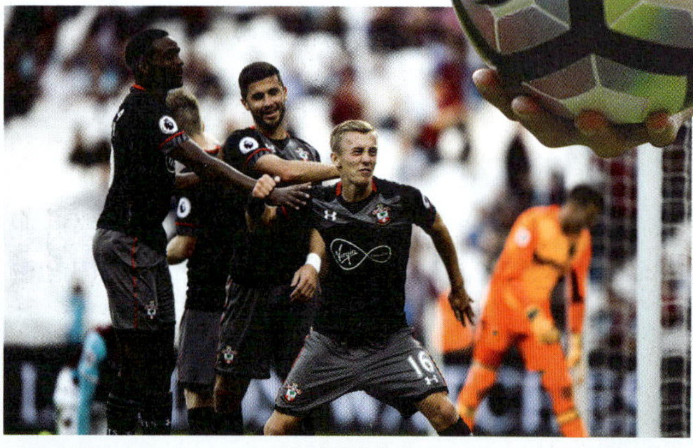

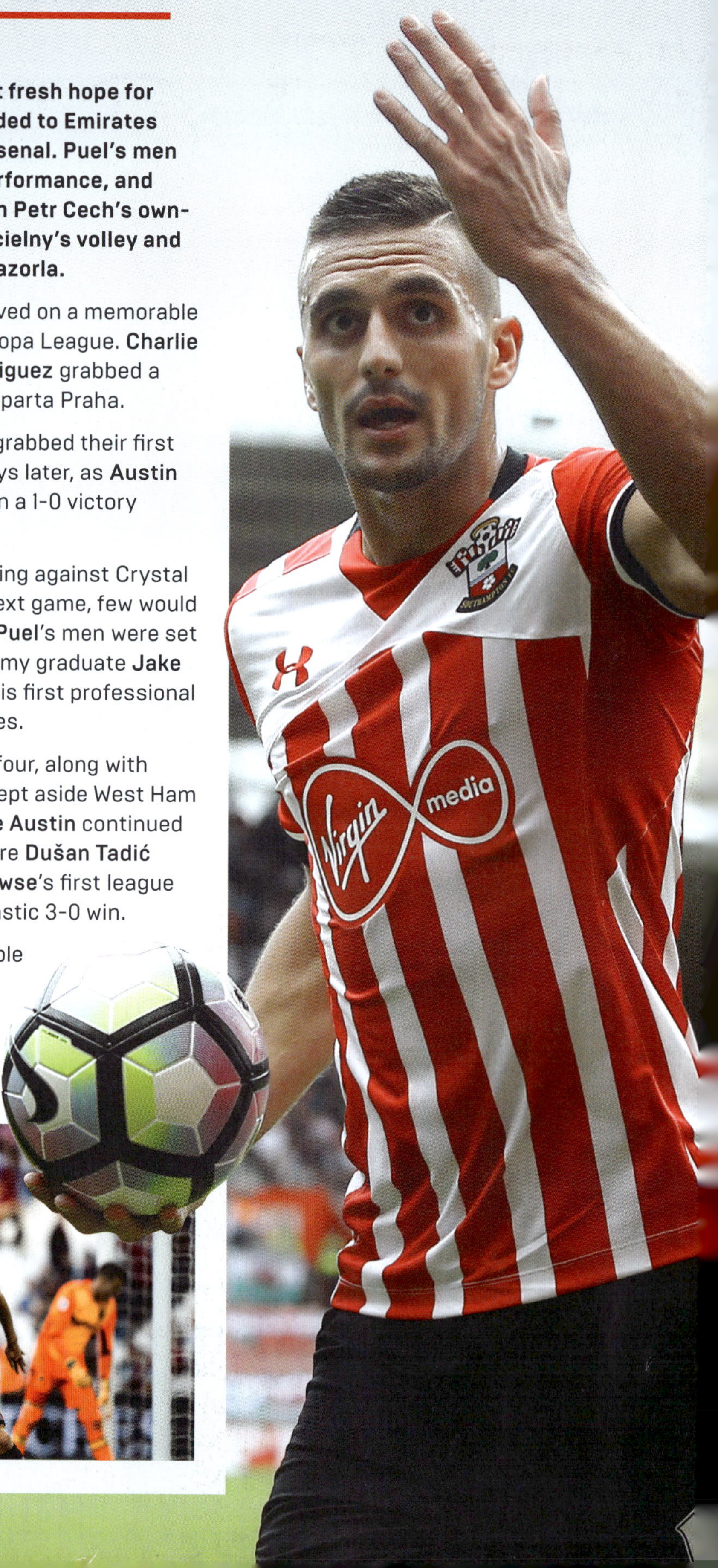

REVIEW

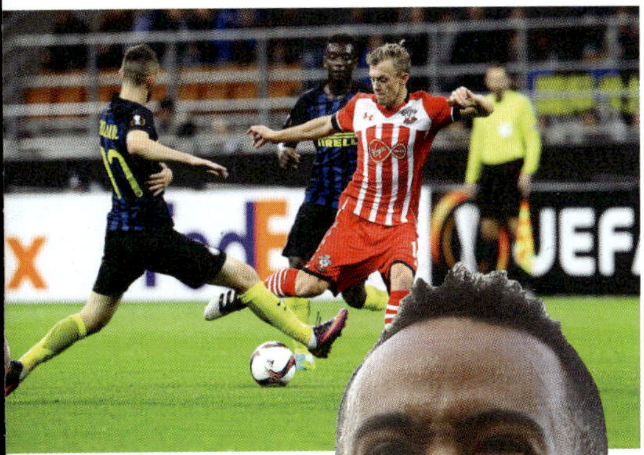

OCTOBER

Saints kicked off October with a visit to reigning champions Leicester City, recording a sixth clean sheet in a row, as they drew 0-0 with the Foxes.

After the second international break of the season, Saints returned with a strong home win against Burnley. **Charlie Austin** scored twice against his former club, with **Nathan Redmond** grabbing his second of the campaign in a 3-1 win.

Next up was a trip to the San Siro! Italian giants Internazionale stood in the way of Saints extending their unbeaten run. Despite dominating, in front of an incredible 6,715 Saints fans, **Antonio Candreva**'s goal was enough to win it for Inter.

A return to Premier League action saw Saints extend their unbeaten league run to five, as they drew 1-1 with Manchester City away from home. **Redmond** handed the visitors the lead, but **Kelechi Iheanacho** earned the hosts a share of the spoils.

Summer signing **Sofiane Boufal**, who had made his debut at the San Siro, showed fans what he was all about with what proved to be the club's Goal of the Season in a 1-0 win against Sunderland in the EFL Cup. Controlling a long ball over the top beautifully, the Moroccan then curled a strike into the top corner, winning the game for Saints.

The month ended with a tricky home clash against Chelsea. **Eden Hazard** fired the visitors ahead early on, before a powerful finish from **Diego Costa** condemned Saints to defeat.

SEASON

NOVEMBER

Having dominated in the San Siro, Saints were intent on getting revenge against Internazionale at St Mary's. After Dušan Tadić had missed a penalty and Mauro Icardi had put the visitors ahead, it looked like it may be more frustration for Puel's side. But skipper Virgil van Dijk led by example to equalise, before an own-goal from Yuto Nagatomo won it for Saints to seal a memorable night.

Saints headed to Hull City for their next Premier League clash, and took an early lead through **Charlie Austin**'s penalty, but quick-fire goals from **Robert Snodgrass** and **Michael Dawson** earned the Tigers victory.

A 0-0 draw with Liverpool followed the November international break, before a disappointing 1-0 defeat to Sparta Praha in the Europa League left Saints needing a win or goalless draw in their final group game to qualify for the knockout stages.

The return of former boss **Ronald Koeman** followed that defeat, and Saints recorded a narrow 1-0 win of their own thanks to **Austin**'s first-minute goal. **Josh Sims**, making his debut, grabbed the assist and put in a man-of-the-match performance.

Saints marched on in the EFL Cup in their final game of the month, as goals from **Jordy Clasie** – his first for the club – and **Ryan Bertrand** sealed a fantastic 2-0 win against Arsenal at Emirates Stadium.

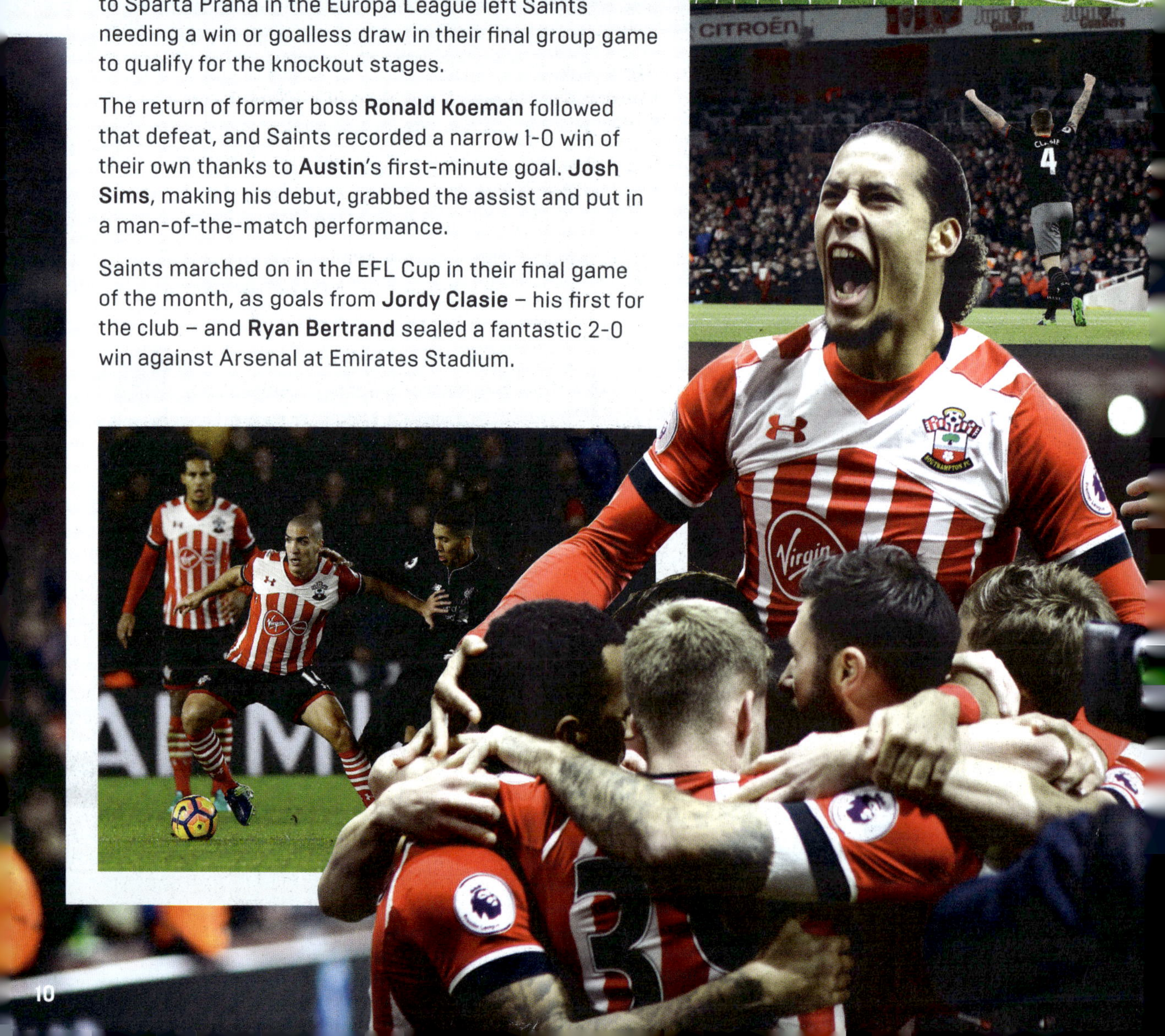

DECEMBER

December would start in disappointing fashion for Saints, as they lost 3-0 at Crystal Palace, before a 1-1 draw with Hapoel Be'er Sheva at St Mary's meant the Israeli side progressed in the Europa League at the expense of Puel's men. Saints would also lose top scorer Charlie Austin to a serious shoulder injury.

Sofiane Boufal's second stunning goal of the season earned Saints a morale-boosting 1-0 win against Middlesbrough at St Mary's in their next fixture, which was followed by a goalless draw against ten-man Stoke City at the Britannia Stadium.

Saints' final game before Christmas saw them travel to south coast rivals AFC Bournemouth. **Nathan Aké** put the hosts ahead, but **Ryan Bertrand**'s equaliser ensured it was level at the break. **Jay Rodriguez** stole the show in the second half, netting from close range to make it 2-1, before a stunning volley sealed the win late on.

The year ended in frustration for Saints, as they were beaten by both Tottenham Hotspur and West Bromwich Albion at St Mary's. Despite **Virgil van Dijk**'s early opener against Spurs, former boss Mauricio Pochettino's side proved too strong, as **Dele Alli, Harry Kane and Son Heung-Min** all scored in a 4-1 win for the visitors.

Shane Long would also put Saints ahead against West Brom in their final game of 2017, but goals from **Matt Phillips** and **Hal Robson-Kanu** completed the turnaround for the Baggies.

SEASON

JANUARY

Saints headed to Goodison Park for a second clash with former boss Ronald Koeman to start the year, but they were left disappointed on this occasion, as second half goals from Enner Valencia, Leighton Baines and Romelu Lukaku earned Everton a 3-0 win.

After a 2-2 draw with Norwich City in the third round of the Emirates FA Cup, Saints took on Liverpool at St Mary's in the first leg of their EFL Cup semi-final clash. **Nathan Redmond**'s first half-goal provided **Puel**'s side with the advantage ahead of the second leg at Anfield two weeks later.

Saints' disappointing run in the league continued, however, as they lost 1-0 at Burnley, before progressing in the FA Cup thanks to **Shane Long**'s late winner against Norwich in the replay.

A 3-0 league success against Leicester City, thanks to goals from **James Ward-Prowse**, **Jay Rodriguez** and **Dušan Tadić** was the perfect tonic ahead of the second leg against Liverpool, which would prove to be one of Saints' most memorable nights in recent history.

A terrific defensive display kept Saints ahead in the tie, before **Long** sparked magical scenes in the away end with a late winner on the night, securing a 2-0 success overall and a place in the final at Wembley.

Saints' run in the other domestic cup competition, the FA Cup, would end at the fourth-round stage, as Arsenal won 5-0 at St Mary's, before a 2-1 defeat at Swansea City ended a month of highs and lows.

Off the pitch, **José Fonte**'s Saints career would come to an end, as the captain made the move to West Ham United following an excellent seven-year stay, while Saints completed the signing of Italian **Manolo Gabbiadini** on deadline day.

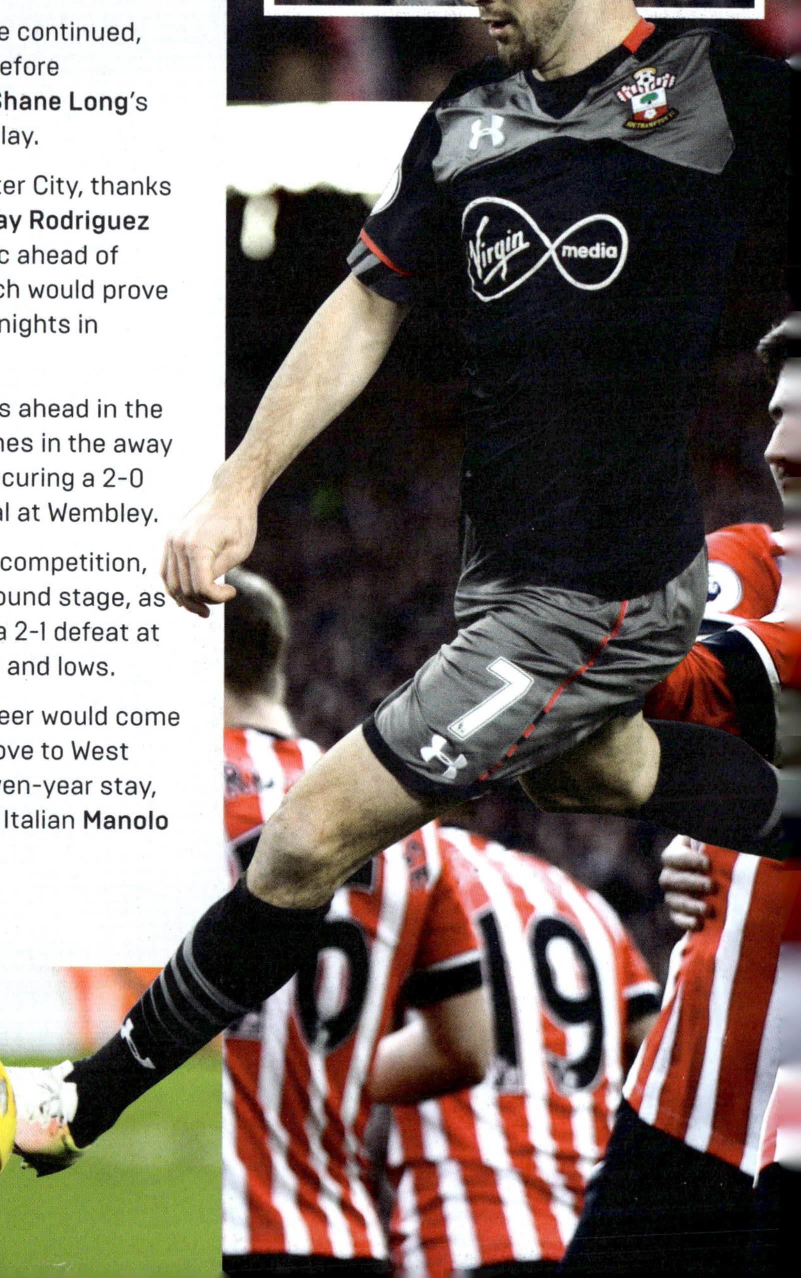

REVIEW

FEBRUARY

Manolo Gabbiadini made a stunning start to life at St Mary's, netting a powerful opener to give Saints the lead against José Fonte's West Ham. But the Hammers would fight back through goals from Pedro Obiang, Andy Carroll and Mark Noble.

Gabbiadini would net again in his first away game for Saints, grabbing two in a fine 4-0 win against Sunderland at the Stadium of Light. His double set **Puel**'s side on their way, before a **Jason Denayer** own-goal and **Shane Long** strike rounded off the win.

The month would end with Saints' first major final since 2003, as they took on Manchester United in the EFL Cup final at Wembley. Backed by incredible support from the Saints faithful, **Gabbiadini** thought he'd given Saints the lead, only for his effort to be incorrectly ruled out for offside.

United would take advantage, going two goals ahead through **Zlatan Ibrahimović** and **Jesse Lingard**, but **Gabbiadini** would not be denied just before half time, as he pulled one back for Saints.

The Italian then levelled proceedings with his fifth goal in three games, sparking wild celebrations in the Southampton end. **Puel**'s men continued to dominate, but were left heartbroken when **Ibrahimović** headed home a late winner for **José Mourinho**'s side.

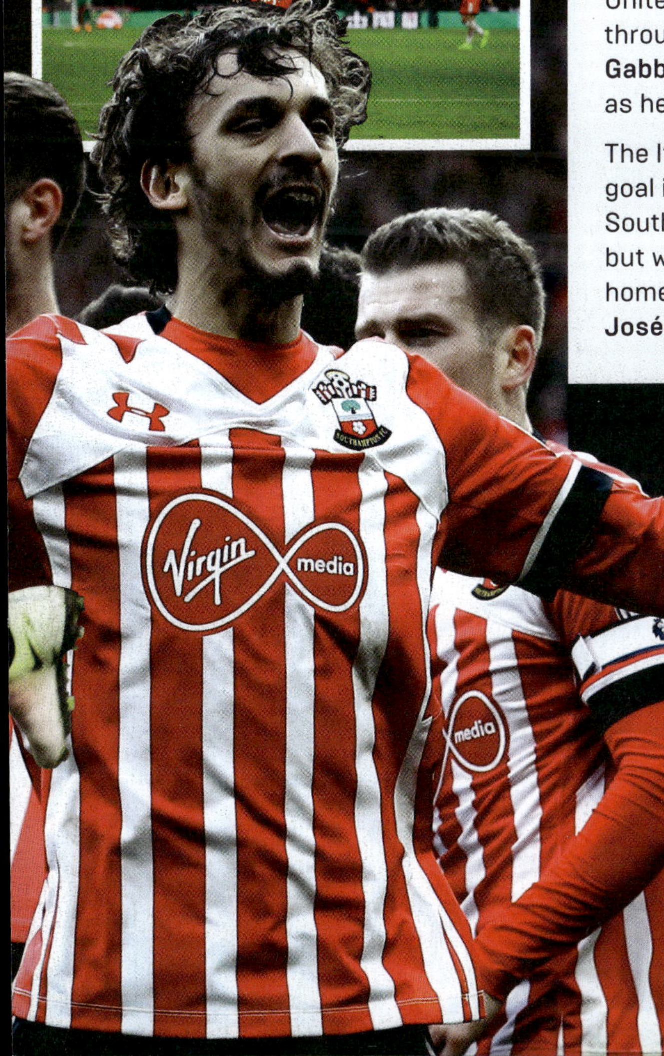

SEASON

MARCH

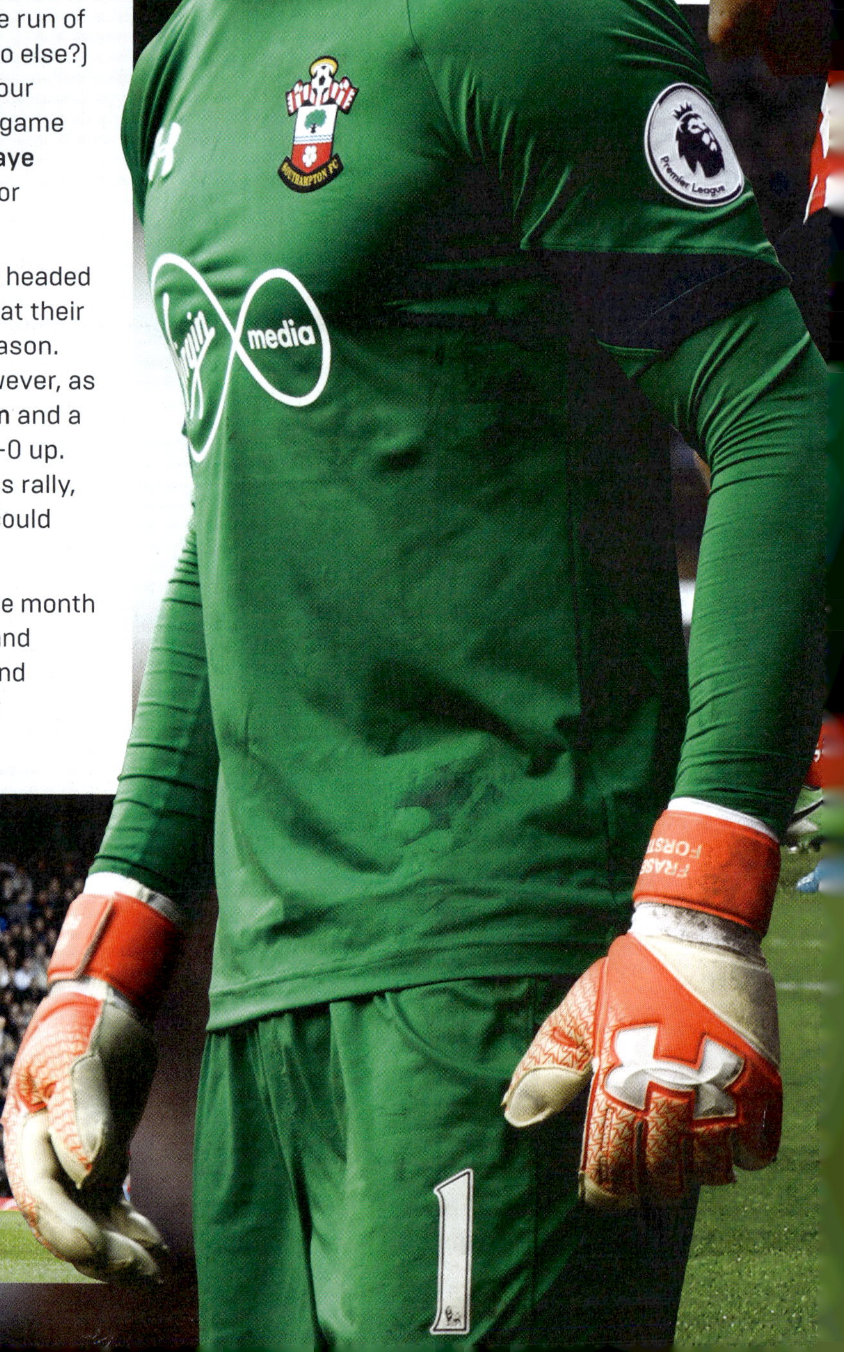

Saints returned from EFL Cup heartbreak with a trip to Watford in the Premier League. After falling behind to **Troy Deeney**'s strike early on, Saints were ahead at the break thanks to goals from **Nathan Redmond** and **Dušan Tadić**.

Stefano Okaka levelled against the run of play, before **Manolo Gabbiadini** (who else?) made it 3-2 with his sixth goal in four games. **Redmond**'s second of the game made the win safe, before **Abdoulaye Doucouré** grabbed a consolation for Watford, making it 4-3.

After another free weekend, Saints headed to White Hart Lane, hoping to repeat their winning performance from last season. They would be unable to do so however, as a fine strike from **Christian Eriksen** and a penalty from **Dele Alli** put Spurs 2-0 up. **James Ward-Prowse** led the Saints rally, pulling one back, but the visitors could not find an equaliser.

There would be a positive end to the month for Saints, as both **Ward-Prowse** and **Redmond** made their senior England debuts in the Three Lions' friendly against Germany.

REVIEW
APRIL

Harry Arter's late penalty miss ensured Saints of a point at home against south coast rivals AFC Bournemouth, before a comeback win against Crystal Palace, again at St Mary's, made it four points from two at the start of April.

Christian Benteke gave the Eagles the lead under the lights at St Mary's, but goals from **Nathan Redmond**, **Maya Yoshida** and **James Ward-Prowse** saw Saints fight back to claim a vital three points.

Saints would make it three games unbeaten inside a week as they secured another important win at West Bromwich Albion to close the gap on the eighth-placed Baggies. **Jordy Clasie**'s excellent strike was the difference between the two, as Saints won 1-0 at the Hawthorns.

Defeats to Champions League chasing Manchester City and eventual champions Chelsea would follow, however. Against City, second half goals from **Vincent Kompany**, **Leroy Sané** and **Sergio Agüero** condemned Saints to a 3-0 defeat.

At Stamford Bridge in the following fixture, **Eden Hazard** netted early for Chelsea, before **Oriol Romeu** equalised against his former club. A goal from **Gary Cahill** just before half time restored Chelsea's lead, with a brace from **Diego Costa** in the second half making it 4-1. **Ryan Bertrand** also grabbed a goal against his former club, making it 4-2, but it was too little, too late for Saints.

April ended with a frustrating 0-0 draw at home to Hull City. Neither side could find the breakthrough, though Saints were handed the chance to win it from the penalty spot in stoppage time. **Dušan Tadić** was denied though, as the Tigers held on for a share of the spoils.

SEASON

MAY

The final month of the campaign kicked off at Anfield, as Saints made it four unbeaten and four clean sheets against Liverpool over the course of the season. Fraser Forster was the hero, saving James Milner's penalty to earn a respectable draw for Puel's side.

After a 2-0 defeat at home to Arsenal, with goals from **Alexis Sanchez** and **Olivier Giroud** proving the difference, Saints picked up three points in their final away game of the campaign at Middlesbrough.

Jay Rodriguez and **Nathan Redmond** scored to give Saints a two-goal advantage. After **Shane Long** had missed the chance to make it three from the penalty spot, **Patrick Bamford** pulled one back. Saints would hold on though, picking up a vital three points in the race for eighth.

Revenge against Manchester United was on the menu for Saints in their penultimate game of the season. Striker **Manolo Gabbiadini** failed to convert from the penalty spot early on, as **Sergio Romero** saved, with neither side then able to find the breakthrough as the game finished goalless.

The season drew to a close at home to Stoke City, and despite a 1-0 defeat to the Potters, results elsewhere ensured Saints of their fourth consecutive top-eight finish in the Premier League.

Heading home after reaching Wembley!

We see you, Redderz!

Live long and prosper, Prowsey!

Nice stabilisers, Charlie!

Prowsey likes his programme cover!

Thank you, Longy!

Stick to the football, boys!

BEHIND THE SCENES

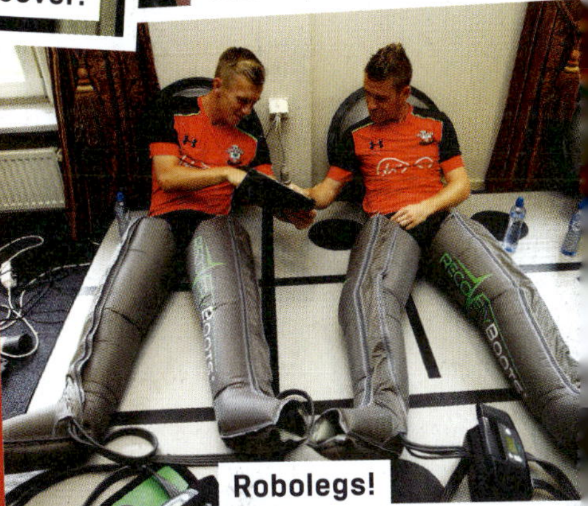
Robolegs!

Looking sharp, Jack!

Franny Benali's back!

Manolo Gabbiadini and a Lamborghini!

Hey there, Charlie!

Harry and Sam in the festive spirit!

Oriol Romeooooooooh!

EFL Cup Final

It may not have been the ending everyone connected with Southampton Football Club had hoped for, but the club's trip to Wembley for their first major final since 2003 will live long in the memory of every Saints supporter.

After a stunning run to the final of the EFL Cup, in which Saints kept five clean sheets while beating four Premier League teams, Manchester United stood in the way of glory at Wembley.

In front of an incredibly loud and supportive 32,000 Saints fans, the players gave absolutely everything, dominating against the Red Devils for long periods of the match, but ultimately falling just short of lifting the trophy.

Manolo Gabbiadini's double saw Saints come back from two goals behind, with the Italian's equaliser sparking wild scenes in the Southampton end, but a second goal for Zlatan Ibrahimović late on won it for José Mourinho's side, breaking the hearts of every Saints supporter in the stadium.

While Saints may not have come away with the trophy, the spirit, passion and support shown made it a day for everyone connected with Southampton Football Club to be proud of.

Here, we take a look back at some of the best photos from an unforgettable afternoon at Wembley...

REDMOND
22
20

sky

ENERGY DRINK
EFL

media

Player Awards

Southampton Football Club held its annual Player Awards ceremony on a glittering night at St Mary's.

There was no doubt who the night belonged to, with midfielder Oriol Romeu capping an incredible individual season by winning both of the big prizes.

Here, we take a look at who claimed all of the prestigious awards...

PLAYERS' PLAYER OF THE SEASON

As well as being recognised by the club's supporters, Oriol Romeu was also the resounding winner of the vote from his Southampton teammates, as an overwhelming majority of the first-team players chose the midfielder as their standout performer.

"It has been an amazing season, I've enjoyed it a lot, and I've felt everyone's support," said Romeu. "I need to thank my teammates, because they've valued my work ever since I came here. They've awarded me with this, and I couldn't be any happier."

FANS' PLAYER OF THE SEASON

The big award of the night went to Oriol Romeu, as the midfielder won the supporters' vote in a landslide.

Romeu's dominant performances established him as a firm favourite with the club's fans, and that appreciation was reciprocated by the 25-year-old.

"It's special not only because of this award," he said. "Every game, every simple moment, you walk on the streets and they really appreciate the work that not only me, but all of us, are doing and that's something very enjoyable."

PRESIDENT'S CHOICE AWARD

Each season, honorary club president and Saints' record appearance holder, Terry Paine, selects his player of the season.

Paine often opts to select one of the more unsung members of the team, and it is fair to say his choice this year was one of the most popular yet, as he picked Maya Yoshida as the recipient of the prize.

Paine explained: "He has performed extraordinarily well. I think he's been very impressive."

Yoshida said: "I am very happy to get this prize and really appreciate everyone I work with at this club."

SCHOLAR OF THE SEASON

Jake Vokins was the proud recipient of the Southampton Academy's award, capping a fine year for him, and marking him out as yet another potential star left-back to emerge from the youth ranks at St Mary's.

The 17-year-old, who has been with the club since the age of eight, has impressed for both the Under-18s and Under-23s.

He said: "I'm absolutely delighted to win this award. I'm really looking forward to seeing what the future holds and all the success the club can bring me and I can bring them."

GOAL OF THE SEASON

In one of the closest votes we have seen, Sofiane Boufal edged out Jay Rodriguez for the prestigious honour.

Boufal had two efforts on the shortlist for the prize, but it was his wonder strike in the 1-0 EFL Cup win over Sunderland that won it.

Boufal was nearly beaten by Rodriguez though, with his spectacular volley in the 3-1 win at Bournemouth going close to topping the poll, garnering 29.3 per cent of the votes compared to Boufal's 31.3 per cent.

GIRLS' REGIONAL TALENT CLUB PLAYER OF THE SEASON

A new award for 2017 saw Phoebe Williams claim the Girls' Regional Talent Club Player of the Season prize.

Saints' Regional Talent Club was set up only a year earlier, and has gone from strength to strength in that time, with Phoebe one of a number of international players in the ranks.

Phoebe said: "I'm very proud and very happy. It's good that women's football is getting so big at Southampton."

QUIZ OF TH

1. Who wore the number one shirt, for the first time since joining Saints, during the 2016/17 campaign?

2. Who scored Saints' first goal of the 2016/17 season?

3. Which player provided the most Premier League assists during 2016/17?

4. Can you name the player who made the most substitute appearances last season?

5. Who set up Shane Long for the winning goal away to Liverpool in the EFL Cup semi-final second leg?

▲ Shane Long scores a special goal against Liverpool, but whose pass is he converting?

6. Can you name the two players who finished as Saints' top scorers in the 2016/17 Europa League group stages?

7. Who scored Southampton's first goal of 2017?

▼ Manolo Gabbiadini celebrates his first Southampton goal, but how many more followed?

10

8. Forster; Cédric, Yoshida, Bertrand, Ward-Prowse, Davis, Redmond, Tadić, Gabbiadini. Which two players are missing from the EFL Cup final starting line-up?

9. How many clean sheets did Southampton keep against Liverpool in 2016/17?

10. How many goals did Manolo Gabbiadini score in his first four matches?

E SEASON

11 Which player wore the number 19 shirt during the 2016/17 season?

12 How many Academy graduates featured throughout the previous campaign?

13 Who won the President's Choice Award at the 2016/17 Player Awards night?

14 Who scored their first Premier League goal in a 1-0 win against West Brom in April 2017?

15 Two players scored goals against both Middlesbrough and Sunderland in 2016/17. Who were they?

16 Southampton's trip to Wembley for the EFL Cup final in February 2017 was their first major final since when?

▼ Saints fans cheer their team at the EFL Cup final - their first major final since when?

16

▼ Saints celebrate a clean sheet at Arsenal, but how many more did they get on the way to the EFL Cup final?

20

17 How many league clean sheets did Southampton keep during the 2016/17 campaign?

18 Can you name the two Saints players who scored against their former club when Saints took on Chelsea at Stamford Bridge in April 2017?

19 Who was named Club Captain following José Fonte's move to West Ham United?

20 How many clean sheets did Saints keep on their way to the EFL Cup final?

Answers on page 62-63

TOP FIVE GOALS

1 SOFIANE BOUFAL
vs Sunderland (H)

An otherwise uneventful EFL Cup game was spectacularly lit up by Boufal sensationally controlling a ball that dropped high out of the sky, then cutting inside on the corner of the area and arcing a glorious shot into the far top corner, clipping the bar on the way in.

2 SHANE LONG
vs Liverpool (A)

Long sealed Saints' place in the EFL Cup final with a goal that will live long in the memory. Josh Sims ran the length of the Anfield pitch, before sliding the ball to him down the inside-right. Long's first touch was perfect and his finish across goal emphatic.

3 JAY RODRIGUEZ
vs Bournemouth (A)

Rodriguez had already put Saints ahead at the Vitality Stadium when a loose, bouncing ball broke his way 20 yards out. With his back to goal, he swivelled elegantly on the spot and crashed a dipping right-footed volley into the top corner.

4 DUŠAN TADIĆ
vs West Ham (A)

A simply sublime team goal ended with Charlie Austin's first-time pass picking out Tadić's run through the middle. He then produced a wonderful dummy to fool West Ham keeper Adrián, allowing him to roll the ball into an empty net.

5 SOFIANE BOUFAL
vs Middlesbrough (H)

Another phenomenal Boufal goal won this game. Receiving a pass from James Ward-Prowse 25 yards out, he spun superbly to beat his man, before lashing a swerving, left-footed shot that flew into the top corner, leaving the keeper rooted to the spot.

TOP FIVE GAMES

① Southampton 2-1 Internazionale

A special night at St Mary's saw Saints beat one of Europe's giants in the UEFA Europa League. Mauro Icardi's first-half goal and Dušan Tadić's penalty miss meant frustration at the break, but Virgil van Dijk slammed home from close range in the 64th minute to level, before Yuto Nagatomo's own-goal shortly after sent the home crowd wild.

② Liverpool 0-1 Southampton

Another night that will live long in the memory of Southampton supporters. Holding a slender 1-0 advantage from the first leg of their EFL Cup semi-final, Saints still went to Anfield as underdogs. An incredible Fraser Forster save in the second half kept them ahead before Josh Sims teed up Shane Long at the end to seal a Wembley spot.

③ Watford 3-4 Southampton

This back-and-forth game at Vicarage Road could arguably be claimed as the most entertaining of the season. Saints were 2-1 up at half-time, as Nathan Redmond and Dušan Tadić netted following Troy Deeney's opener. Stefano Okaka equalised late on, but Manolo Gabbiadini and another Redmond effort made it 4-2, before Abdoulaye Doucouré's late strike.

④ Southampton 3-0 Leicester

Saints demolished the reigning Premier League champions with one of their best displays of the season. James Ward-Prowse's superb strike across goal set them on their way, before Jay Rodriguez lashed home from a tight angle to make it 2-0 before half-time. Dušan Tadić's late penalty then completed the rout.

⑤ West Ham 0-3 Southampton

Saints' first trip to London Stadium saw them produce one of their finest away performances of the campaign. Charlie Austin stroked in Ryan Bertrand's cutback to make it 1-0, before Dušan Tadić capped a slick team move by dummying West Ham keeper Adrián to make it 2-0. James Ward-Prowse then fired home in the closing stages for the third.

TOP FIVE ASSISTS

1 JOSH SIMS
vs Liverpool (A) (EFL Cup)

This stunning assist for Shane Long from the teenager not only tops the list because of its importance, as it sealed Saints' trip to the EFL Cup final, it's also in this position because of its quality. Sims broke nearly the full length of the Anfield pitch, before sliding a beautifully-weighted pass down the inside-right channel for Long to slam home and send the visiting fans wild.

2 STEVEN DAVIS
vs Bournemouth (A)

Davis set up Jay Rodriguez for the simplest of goals – and what proved to be the decisive one – in Southampton's 3-1 win at Bournemouth with this sensational assist. Davis played a slick one-two with Sofiane Boufal to burst behind the Cherries defence, before lifting the ball over keeper Artur Boruc and a sliding Steve Cook for Rodriguez to slide in and convert.

3 CHARLIE AUSTIN
vs West Ham (A)

Almost without looking, Austin produced a sublime, first-time pass with his left foot to split West Ham's defence at London Stadium and send Dušan Tadić clean through on goal. The Serbian then did the rest to cap a stunning team move, as he dummied his way past Hammers keeper Adrián before rolling the ball into an empty net.

4 JAY RODRIGUEZ
vs West Ham (H)

Receiving a pass from Oriol Romeu on the halfway line with his back to goal, Rodriguez spun, looked up, and chipped an inch-perfect ball over the West Ham defence for Manolo Gabbiadini to run onto. The Italian did the rest, smashing home on his debut for the club to kick-start a record-breaking scoring run.

5 SHANE LONG
vs Middlesbrough (A)

When Long raced onto a ball down the right channel at the Riverside Stadium, there appeared little in the way of options for him. But he pivoted superbly to cut a perfectly-weighted ball back towards the penalty spot, right into the path of Jay Rodriguez. The forward made no mistake, hammering in a low half-volley to set Saints on the way to victory.

MANOLO'S MAGIC MONTH

WHEN SOUTHAMPTON COMPLETED THE SIGNING OF STRIKER MANOLO GABBIADINI ON 1ST FEBRUARY 2017, FEW COULD HAVE PREDICTED JUST HOW MUCH OF AN IMPACT HE WOULD HAVE.

The Italian, who joined the club from Napoli, scored within 12 minutes of his debut, as he fired in a spectacular strike against West Ham, although Saints would subsequently lose the match 3-1.

It was to be the start of a magical month for the 25-year-old, who went on a record-breaking run.

Gabbiadini's next match was the Premier League trip to Sunderland, and it didn't take him long to shine on a dreary day in the north east.

The forward got his first of two goals with a sharp near-post run to meet Ryan Bertrand's cross after half-an-hour, before he produced a sensational turn in the area right on half-time to baffle a couple of Sunderland defenders before rolling the ball past keeper Vito Mannone.

Even Manchester United couldn't stop his incredible scoring feats, as he netted twice – well, let's be honest, three times – in the EFL Cup final, at Wembley.

After having a goal incorrectly ruled out for offside when the score was 0-0, Gabbiadini scored twice after United had gone 2-0 up to level the match, prodding in a James Ward-Prowse cross just before half-time and then hitting a stunning half-volley on the turn inside the area shortly after the break. Unfortunately, United would win 3-2, but it was still a stunning display from the striker.

Saints then went to Watford in their next game, with Gabbiadini alertly taking advantage of a mistake from keeper Heurelho Gomes to put his side 3-2 up in a game they would win 4-3.

It made it six goals in his first four games for Southampton and set a new club record, as Gabbiadini became the first ever Saints player to score in his first three Premier League matches!

2017/18 JUNIOR MEMBERSHIP

From **£10**

11-16 year olds | 4-10 year olds | 0-3 year olds

2017/18 Junior Members will benefit from an enhanced Welcome Pack this season, as well as additional mailings through the year, priority ticket access and much more. We've created three age bands to ensure you get more out of your Junior Membership than ever before.

southamptonfc.com | 02381 780 780 | Visit the Ticket Office

SAINTS PUZZLES

CAN YOU ANSWER ALL 13 QUESTIONS CORRECTLY TO UNLOCK THE ANSWER?

1/ Which player scored Saints' first & last goals of the season?

2/ Which Saints player was awarded an MBE in June 2017?

3/ Who scored two goals for Saints in the EFL Cup final?

4/ What was Saints' final league position in 2016/17?

5/ Which goalkeeper is sponsored by Under Armour?

6/ Who won the club's Players' Player and Fans' Player of the Season awards in 2016/17?

7/ Who did Saints beat over two legs to reach the EFL Cup final?

8/ Which Academy graduate scored his first senior goal in Saints' 2-0 EFL Cup win against Crystal Palace?

9/ Who is Saints' record appearance holder and also Club President?

10/ Who produces Saints' home and away kits?

11/ Who scored the only goal when Saints beat Manchester United in the 1976 FA Cup final?

12/ What was the name of Saints' ground before they moved to their current stadium?

13/ Who set up a goal inside a minute on his debut for Saints during 2016/17?

FIND THE WORDS IN THE GRID.

Words can go horizontally, vertically and diagonally in all eight directions.

ACADEMY
BOUFAL
FORSTER
GABBIADINI
GOAL
HEROES
LEAGUE
LETISSIER
ROMEU
SAMMYSAINT
STAPLEWOOD
UNDERARMOUR

R	I	W	S	M	H	G	D	F	W	R	Y	H
E	R	N	M	T	L	N	M	N	D	N	T	E
T	U	J	I	Z	A	K	H	L	K	N	D	R
S	O	N	Y	D	B	P	L	V	I	Q	B	O
R	M	N	L	T	A	R	L	A	C	O	D	E
O	R	Q	P	E	W	I	S	E	U	X	B	S
F	A	H	H	H	T	Y	B	F	W	P	L	Y
N	R	L	Y	F	M	I	A	B	T	O	M	K
W	E	K	T	M	D	L	S	Z	A	E	O	M
K	D	H	A	B	V	K	R	S	D	G	K	D
H	N	S	M	G	O	A	L	A	I	N	M	M
K	U	R	O	M	E	U	C	G	X	E	N	R
B	G	L	E	U	G	A	E	L	L	N	R	X

Answers on page 60-6

MEET THE **NEW BOYS**

JAN BEDNAREK

POSITION: DEFENDER
DATE OF BIRTH: 12/04/1996
NATIONALITY: POLISH
FORMER CLUBS: LECH POZNAŃ, GÓRNIK ŁĘCZNA (LOAN)
HEIGHT: 189CM
WEIGHT: 77KG

Football, and in particular trying to stop the opposition from scoring, clearly runs in the Bednarek family! Jan's older brother Filip is also a professional footballer, who is currently playing for Dutch Eerste Divisie side De Graafschap. While Jan plays as a defender, Filip is a goalkeeper. Saints' new signing credits his brother with having the biggest influence on his career.

Jan has played at every youth level for his country. His first international recognition came at Under-16 level, and the defender has continued to progress through the age groups. In the summer of 2017, Jan featured at the Under-21 European Championships, where his Poland side came up against an England team featuring four Saints players.

Real Madrid and Spain defender Sergio Ramos is the player Jan says inspires him the most in football. The Saints man says he is always watching videos of Ramos, who he believes is the best defender in the world, to try and pick up tips that will help him improve his ability as a player.

Jan once watched a game from the stands with the Lech Poznań fans. Having grown up supporting the club as a child, he decided to experience an away game from a different perspective, when he joined Lech fans in the away end against rivals Legia Warsaw in October 2015. We wonder whether he knew all the chants?

Ever wondered what music the players like to listen to in the changing room to get themselves ready for a match? Well for Jan, it's Polish rap music. The defender is a big fan of the genre, and says it's the best type of music for him to listen to just before kick-off, to make sure he's ready for the game.

MARIO LEMINA

POSITION: MIDFIELDER
DATE OF BIRTH: 01/09/1993
NATIONALITY: GABONESE
FORMER CLUBS: LORIENT, MARSEILLE, JUVENTUS
HEIGHT: 184CM
WEIGHT: 85KG

Mario Lemina was born in Gabon, but began his playing career in France. The central midfielder joined French side Lorient at the age of 11, working his way through the club's academy before going on to play for the first team during the 2012/13 campaign. His impressive performances earned him a move to Marseille at the end of that season.

Having lived in France for a number of years, Lemina was able to represent them at youth level. The midfielder featured at the 2013 FIFA Under-20 World Cup, playing alongside the likes of Paul Pogba, as France won the competition, beating Uruguay in the final.

Saints were linked with Lemina back in 2015, but on that occasion the midfielder made a loan switch from Marseille to Juventus in Italy. His two years with the Old Lady would prove to be extremely successful, as Lemina lifted the Serie A title and the Coppa Italia in both 2016 and 2017, before sealing a switch to the Premier League with Saints.

Despite playing for France at youth level, Lemina opted to represent Gabon, his country of birth, at senior level. Lemina featured for Gabon at the 2017 Africa Cup of Nations, while the midfielder has featured heavily in Gabon's 2018 FIFA World Cup qualifying matches.

Lemina will be coming up against some familiar faces in the Premier League. During his time at Marseille, the midfielder played alongside Michy Batshuayi, Benjamin Mendy, Andre Ayew and Giannelli Imbula. Lemina was teammates with Paul Pogba, Alvaro Morata and former Saints defender Martin Cáceres during his spell with Juventus.

MEET THE **NEW BOYS**

WESLEY HOEDT

POSITION: DEFENDER
DATE OF BIRTH: 06/03/1994
NATIONALITY: DUTCH
FORMER CLUBS: HVV HOLLANDIA, AZ, LAZIO
HEIGHT: 192CM
WEIGHT: 77KG

Born in Alkmaar in March 1994, Hoedt joined AZ's youth academy at the age of 11, progressing through the age groups before making his professional debut for his local club in a Europa League game against PAOK in December 2013. He would go on to make 30 appearances for his local club before making the move to Lazio.

Hoedt has represented the Netherlands at both youth and senior level. The defender featured for the Dutch Under-15s, Under-20s and Under-21s before winning his first senior cap in March 2017, coming on as a substitute in a 2-0 defeat against Bulgaria. He made his first start three days later in a game against Italy, playing the full 90 minutes.

There will be some familiar faces for Hoedt at Southampton. The defender came up against both Mario Lemina and Manolo Gabbiadini during his time in Serie A with Lazio. He will also be able to call on the support of fellow countrymen Jordy Clasie and Virgil van Dijk as he settles in to life at St Mary's.

At 6ft 4in, it's hardly surprising that Hoedt is a threat at set pieces in the opposition penalty area. The defender has scored six goals so far in his career, including four during his time with Lazio. The Dutchman also netted twice in his 25 Eredivisie appearances for AZ Alkmaar.

Hoedt lifted his first piece of silverware as a professional shortly before making the move to Southampton. The defender was part of the Lazio squad that beat Italian champions Juventus 3-2 to win the 2017 Supercoppa Italiana, at the Stadio Olimpico in Rome.

MEET THE NEW BOSS

SOUTHAMPTON HAVE A NEW MANAGER FOR THE 2017/18 SEASON, WITH **MAURICIO PELLEGRINO** THE MAN IN CHARGE! HERE ARE FIVE FACTS YOU SHOULD KNOW ABOUT HIM, AS WELL AS A FACTFILE.

1 He cut his teeth in coaching under Rafa Benítez

After a spell working with the youth team at Valencia, Pellegrino got his first big break in coaching when Benítez added him to his staff at Liverpool. He then followed Benítez to Internazionale in 2010, before his first management job, at Valencia, two years later.

2 He led Alavés to one of the best seasons in their history

Taking over the newly-promoted side last summer, he guided the Spanish club to a ninth-place finish in La Liga – a position they have bettered only three times in their history, and took them to their first ever Copa del Rey final.

3 He played under Louis van Gaal and José Mourinho at Barcelona

Then Barca boss van Gaal loaned the Argentinian centre-back in 1998/99. Current Manchester United boss Mourinho was on van Gaal's coaching staff at the time, while he played alongside greats such as Pep Guardiola, Luís Figo and Rivaldo, helping the Catalan club to the La Liga title.

4 Former Southampton boss Mauricio Pochettino is one of his friends

Pochettino, who took charge of Saints from January 2013 until the summer of 2014, and Pellegrino both hail from Argentina and know each other well. The pair both played in Spain and went on the same coaching course when they were making the transition towards management.

5 He had great success as a player

Pellegrino began his career in Argentina with Vélez Sarsfield, going on to play for Barcelona, Valenica, Liverpool and Alavés. He won three La Liga titles – one with Barca, two with Valencia – and also won the UEFA Cup with Valencia, while featuring in two Champions League finals.

FACTFILE

Date of birth: 5th October 1971

Place of birth: Leones, Argentina

Playing position: Centre back

Playing career: Vélez Sarsfield, Barcelona (loan), Valencia, Liverpool, Alavés.

Teams managed: Valencia (2012), Estudiantes (2013-15), Independiente (2015-16), Alavés (2016-17)

Playing honours: Argentine Primera División (1993, 1995, 1996, 1998), Copa Libertadores (1994), Intercontinental Cup (1994), La Liga (1999, 2002, 2004), Copa del Rey (1999), UEFA Cup (2004), UEFA Super Cup (2004).

TEAMMATES *WITH CHARLIE AUSTIN*

WHO IS THE MOST INTELLIGENT?

That's **Fraser Forster**, he is extremely intelligent, although when it comes to business smarts it's definitely **Ryan Bertrand**. He's got fingers in all sorts of pies in the business world.

WHO IS THE MOST SKILFUL?

Sofiane Boufal. Nathan Redmond has a lot of tricks, but Boufal is very, very skilful. He does things and you think 'How on earth did you get out of that situation?'

WHO IS THE FUNNIEST?

Big Stu Taylor. He's absolutely great for the lads. You'd want most of your teammates to be like him. He always comes in every day with a smile on his face. He's not a prankster, but his character just lifts everybody.

WHO HAS THE WORST DRESS SENSE?

Oh, **Pierre-Emile Højbjerg**! He comes into the training ground in some bad, bad gear. To be fair, **Oriol** gives him a run for his money, but he wins – all these flarey jeans and things. They're no good.

WHO HAS THE BEST DRESS SENSE?

Cédric. He loves his tight-fitted clothing! He's got some really nice designer gear and it's all tailored or fitted very nicely for himself.

WHO IS THE HARDEST MAN?

I would say **Oriol**, but **Virgil van Dijk** is so tough to play against. I'd say that Oriol is hard, but Virgil is tough. You think you've got half a yard on him, but then boom, he's there.

WHO IS THE BEST TRAINER?

Oriol Romeu... and **James Ward-Prowse**. Both of them give absolutely 100 per cent every single day. Ori, to be fair, you almost can't even call it training – he trains the way he plays, and that's just Oriol.

WHO IS THE BEST DANCER?

Nathan Redmond, without a doubt. He's got some genuinely superb moves. Cuco Martina came close, but Nathan is the best, definitely.

WHO IS THE WORST DANCER?

Oriol! I've seen Oriol's, shall we call them 'moves', out in Dubai and he is hands down the worst dancer. He does some weird stuff!

WHO HAS THE HARDEST SHOT?

Virgil! He has an absolute hammer foot and there is absolutely no back-lift. Fortunately I've never got in the way of one of them, and I don't intend to, but you speak to the keepers and it's definitely him.

WHO HAS THE WORST TASTE IN MUSIC?

Pierre-Emile Højbjerg! It's as bad as his dress sense!

WHO HAS THE BEST TASTE IN MUSIC?

That's a tough one, because there's different likes all over, but I would say **Nathan Redmond**. He's the DJ for us if we go into the gym or the dressing room. There's a bit of dance music in there, a bit of hip hop and rap – modern day stuff.

IF YOU HAD TO BE STUCK ON A DESERT ISLAND WITH ONE OF YOUR TEAMMATES, WHO WOULD IT BE AND WHY?

Big Stu, by far. He is just someone I have got on really well for the year he has been here. He would find a way of making you laugh in any situation you are in, so I'd pick him.

NEW KIT

SOUTHAMPTON CAUSED QUITE A STIR WHEN THEY UNVEILED THEIR SPECTACULAR NEW KITS IN THE SUMMER!

Under Armour's latest efforts have proved enormously popular with the club's supporters – and it's no surprise.

The home strip is modelled on the famous 1980s strip worn by legends such as Kevin Keegan and Mick Channon, while the away kit has a striking black and turquoise striped look.

While the kits themselves are pretty special, the way they were unveiled was just as incredible.

Four Saints players – Manolo Gabbiadini, Maya Yoshida, Ryan Bertrand and Fraser Forster – were turned into animated superheroes and had to track down the new kits after they were stolen!

They were successful in their mission, with the short film proving a huge hit with Saints supporters and football fans around the world, proving that the strips have very much been Made For Heroes!

Here, we bring you some of the best images and behind-the-scenes shots from the kit launch and photoshoot...

Virgin media
SOUTHAMPTON FC
Virgin media
SOUTHAMPTON FOOTBALL CLUB

PLAYER PROFILES

2 CÉDRIC

Position: Defender
Date of birth: 31/08/1991
Previous clubs: Sporting CP, Académica, Sporting B
Joined Saints: 2015
Height: 172cm
Weight: 67kg
Nationality: Portuguese

PROFILE: A EURO 2016 champion with Portugal, Cédric has gone from strength to strength since joining Saints from Sporting CP in the summer of 2015. His pace has proved a real asset for Saints going forward down the right-hand side, while his defensive qualities have also come a long way in his two seasons at St Mary's. Rewarded with a new deal before the start of the 2016/17 campaign, Cédric is a key part of Saints' future plans.

2016/17 KEY STATS: 34 games played, 3 assists, 73 tackles won

2016/17 STANDOUT MOMENT: Cédric's performances in both legs of the EFL Cup semi-final against Liverpool highlighted his defensive progression from when he first arrived at St Mary's. The right-back was strong, confident and committed defensively, while he continued to offer a presence going forward, helping Saints to two 1-0 victories against the Reds.

3 MAYA YOSHIDA

Position: Defender
Date of birth: 24/08/1988
Previous clubs: Nagoya Grampus, VVV-Venlo
Joined Saints: 2012
Height: 189cm
Weight: 78kg
Nationality: Japanese

PROFILE: The 2016/17 campaign was certainly Yoshida's most impressive since joining the club in 2012. The defender stepped up brilliantly to become the leading centre-back after Virgil van Dijk's injury. Now in his sixth season at St Mary's, Yoshida is a key figure in the Saints dressing room and is much loved by supporters for his passion and commitment. The Japan international also captained the club in the absence of Van Dijk and Steven Davis during the 2016/17 campaign.

2016/17 KEY STATS: 37 games played, 253 clearances, 73 interceptions

2016/17 STANDOUT MOMENT: After a fine season, in which he led by example from the heart of defence, in particular during the second half of the campaign, Yoshida picked up the President's Choice Award at the club's Player Awards night. Presented by Club President Terry Paine, Yoshida took home the award, saying: "I am very happy to get this prize and really appreciate everyone I work with at this club."

PLAYER PROFILES

4 JORDY CLASIE

Position: Midfielder
Date of birth: 27/06/1991
Previous clubs: Feyenoord, Excelsior
Joined Saints: 2015
Height: 169cm
Weight: 66kg
Nationality: Dutch

PROFILE: After a stop-start first season in England, Clasie was once again competing for places in the centre of Saints' midfield. Despite his small stature, Clasie has adapted well to life in the Premier League. The 2016/17 season also saw him find his range in front of goal, netting twice in total, including a strike against West Bromwich Albion, which won the club's April Goal of the Month award.

2016/17 KEY STATS: 24 games played, 2 goals, 1 assist

2016/17 STANDOUT MOMENT: Having not found the net during his first season at the club, Clasie's excellent finish in the 2-0 win against Arsenal in the EFL Cup was a moment to savour for the Dutchman. The powerful strike set Saints on their way to an excellent win, which culminated in the club heading to Wembley for the final of the competition.

5 JACK STEPHENS

Position: Defender
Date of birth: 27/01/1994
Previous clubs: Plymouth, Southampton Academy, Swindon Town, Middlesbrough, Coventry City
Joined Saints: 2011
Height: 185cm
Weight: 75kg
Nationality: English

PROFILE: A versatile defensive player, Stephens enjoyed his breakthrough season with Saints during the 2016/17 season. With the ability to play at right-back or in defensive midfield, it was his performances at centre-back where he made his mark. His composure and range of passing have seen him become an excellent ball-playing defender, who will be hoping for much more success on the back of the 2016/17 campaign.

2016/17 KEY STATS: 23 games played, 113 clearances, 30 interceptions

2016/17 STANDOUT MOMENT: After an injury to Virgil van Dijk, Stephens was thrust into the starting line-up for a succession of big matches, including the EFL Cup semi-final second leg against Liverpool. The defender was superb at Anfield, providing a real commanding presence defensively, helping Saints keep a clean sheet to reach the final at Wembley.

7 SHANE LONG

Position: Striker
Date of birth: 22/01/1987
Previous clubs: Cork City, Reading, West Bromwich Albion, Hull City
Joined Saints: 2014
Height: 178cm
Weight: 70kg
Nationality: Irish

PROFILE: A 2014 summer signing, Long has been an important player for Saints during the last three successful seasons. Whether that be playing as the main striker, or as a winger, Long's pace and directness cause plenty of problems for opposition defenders. The Republic of Ireland international is also excellent in the air, as was proved with his powerful headed goal against West Bromwich Albion during the 2016/17 campaign.

2016/17 KEY STATS: 45 games played, 5 goals, 52 total shots

2016/17 STANDOUT MOMENT: No question about this one. Long netted an injury-time winner in the second leg of the EFL Cup semi-final against Liverpool that ensured Saints would be heading to a major final for the first time since 2003. The striker latched on to Josh Sims' pass and smashed the ball into the net, sparking incredible scenes in the away end.

PLAYER PROFILES

8 STEVEN DAVIS

Position: Midfielder
Date of birth: 01/01/1985
Previous clubs: Aston Villa, Fulham, Rangers
Joined Saints: 2012
Height: 173cm
Weight: 70kg
Nationality: Northern Irish

PROFILE: An experienced midfielder, Davis is a key member of Saints' squad. Now Club Captain, Davis's experience and calm nature on the pitch is vital. The Northern Ireland captain is excellent at providing the link between the defensive players and attackers, with his ability to find space and gaps anywhere on the pitch a key feature of his play. The midfielder also possesses brilliant close control.

2016/17 KEY STATS: 40 games played, 35 chances created, 4 assists

2016/17 STANDOUT MOMENT: Having played a key role in Saints' progression since his arrival in 2012, Davis made the step up to Club Captain during the 2016/17 campaign. In the absence of Virgil van Dijk, Davis was the man to lead Saints out at Wembley in the EFL Cup final against Manchester United.

10 CHARLIE AUSTIN

Position: Striker
Date of birth: 05/07/1989
Previous clubs: Kintbury Rangers, Hungerford Town, Poole Town, Swindon Town, Burnley, QPR
Joined Saints: 2016
Height: 188cm
Weight: 84kg
Nationality: English

PROFILE: Having worked his way up from non-league football to the Premier League, one thing has always been clear with Austin – he knows exactly where the goal is. His poacher's instinct was again evident in the first half of the 2016/17 season, as he netted nine goals in all competitions, before suffering a serious shoulder injury. Austin will be hoping to pick up where he left off and make a return to the England set-up.

2016/17 KEY STATS: 21 games played, 9 goals, 42 total shots

2016/17 STANDOUT MOMENT: Having worked his way up from non-league football, netting two goals in Europe will have been a big moment for Austin. The striker's double in the 3-0 win against Sparta Praha in the UEFA Europa League capped a memorable European night for Saints at St Mary's.

11 DUŠAN TADIĆ

Position: Midfielder
Date of birth: 20/11/1988
Previous clubs: FK Vojvodina, FC Groningen, FC Twente
Joined Saints: 2014
Height: 181cm
Weight: 76kg
Nationality: Serbian

PROFILE: A Serbian international, Tadić has built himself a reputation of a clever playmaker. With excellent technique at set pieces and on the ball, Tadić plays a key role in creating chances for Saints' strikers. The former FC Twente man, who signed a new deal ahead of the 2016/17 campaign, can play on either wing or in the role just behind the striker.

2016/17 KEY STATS: 44 games played, 7 assists, 3 goals

2016/17 STANDOUT MOMENT: Tadić's excellent goal in Saints' 3-0 win against West Ham United highlighted the playmaker's composure and calmness. The Serbian international produced a clever dummy to fool the goalkeeper, before rolling the ball into the back of the net to give Saints a two-goal advantage. The strike was named as the club's September Goal of the Month.

PLAYER PROFILES

13 ALEX MCCARTHY

Position: Goalkeeper
Date of birth: 03/12/1989
Previous clubs: Reading, Woking, Aldershot, Cambridge United, Yeovil, Brentford, Leeds, Ipswich, QPR, Crystal Palace
Joined Saints: 2016
Height: 193cm
Weight: 79kg
Nationality: English

PROFILE: A talented and proven goalkeeper, McCarthy joined the club in 2016 to provide competition to Fraser Forster. Having showcased his qualities throughout the Football League and Premier League, McCarthy has an excellent reputation. The goalkeeper earned international recognition during 2016/17, as he was called up to the England squad.

2016/17 KEY STATS: 2 games played, 0 goals conceded, 100% shots saved

2016/17 STANDOUT MOMENT: Injury cut short McCarthy's season, but his debut against his former club, Crystal Palace, in the EFL Cup showed what a fine stopper the Englishman is. McCarthy impressed in both games he played during the season, saving every shot he faced and conceding none.

14 ORIOL ROMEU

Position: Midfielder
Date of birth: 24/09/1991
Previous clubs: FC Barcelona, FC Barcelona B, Chelsea, Valencia, VfB Stuttgart
Joined Saints: 2015
Height: 183cm
Weight: 83kg
Nationality: Spanish

PROFILE: A tough tackling, committed and passionate midfielder, Spaniard Romeu proved himself to be a vital part of the Saints team during the 2016/17 campaign. Formerly with Barcelona, the midfielder also possesses an excellent range of passing and game understanding, which he showed with many commanding performances during his second full season at St Mary's.

2016/17 KEY STATS: 46 games played, 100 tackles won, 84% pass completion

2016/17 STANDOUT MOMENT: Romeu's double award win at the club's 2016/17 Player Awards highlighted what an incredible season the midfielder had enjoyed. The Spaniard picked up both the Players' Player of the Year and Fans' Player of the Year awards to cap what he himself described as his best season in football. His form was rewarded with a new contract midway through the campaign.

16 JAMES WARD-PROWSE

Position: Midfielder
Date of birth: 01/11/1994
Previous clubs: Southampton Academy
Joined Saints: 2003
Height: 173cm
Weight: 66kg
Nationality: English

PROFILE: A product of Southampton's famed Academy, James Ward-Prowse has been a part of the club's first team for a number of years. His development as a midfielder has been excellent, while his set-piece ability is an aspect of his game that many have praised. The 2016/17 campaign saw Ward-Prowse find his range in front of goal for Saints, netting four times in all competitions. The youngster has been a regular for England Under-21s, who he has captained, while he has also featured for the senior side.

2016/17 KEY STATS: 43 games played, 4 goals, 5 assists

2016/17 STANDOUT MOMENT: While his first league goal from open play, which came against West Ham United, was a great moment, there's no doubt that Ward-Prowse's Three Lions debut was his most memorable moment. Having progressed through the club's Academy, the youngster's debut against Germany was a proud evening for so many connected to Saints.

PLAYER PROFILES

17 VIRGIL VAN DIJK

Position: Defender
Date of birth: 08/07/1991
Previous clubs: FC Groningen, Celtic
Joined Saints: 2015
Height: 193cm
Weight: 92kg
Nationality: Dutch

PROFILE: Dutchman van Dijk has gone from strength to strength since his arrival at Southampton, quickly becoming one of the best defenders in the Premier League. With power, confidence and strength, van Dijk is known for giving opposing strikers a tough time, but his ability on the ball has also been a key factor for Saints since his arrival. After José Fonte's depature, van Dijk was named Team Captain at Southampton.

2016/17 KEY STATS: 30 games played, 4 goals, 202 clearances

2016/17 STANDOUT MOMENT: While van Dijk's performances were almost always excellent, before his season was cut short through injury, his captain's display in the famous 2-1 win against Internazionale was a special night for van Dijk and the club. The defender's equaliser sparked great scenes at St Mary's, before Saints grabbed a winner moments later to see off the Italian giants.

19 SOFIANE BOUFAL

Position: Midfielder
Date of birth: 17/09/1993
Previous clubs: Angers, Lille
Joined Saints: 2016
Height: 170cm
Weight: 60kg
Nationality: Moroccan

PROFILE: A player with huge potential, Boufal became Southampton's club record signing when he arrived from French club Lille in the summer of 2016. Having shown his quality in Ligue 1, Boufal's arrival excited Saints supporters, who were looking forward to seeing his trickery and skill at St Mary's. The Moroccan showed glimpses of that quality during an injury-hit first campaign in England. There's definitely more to come from the winger!

2016/17 KEY STATS: 29 games played, 2 goals, 23 chances created

2016/17 STANDOUT MOMENT: Boufal's strike against Sunderland, which went on to win the club's Goal of the Season, was undoubtedly the finest moment of his debut season for Saints. The winger controlled a high ball over the top beautifully, before curling a shot into the top-right hand corner of the net, helping Saints march on in the competition.

20 MANOLO GABBIADINI

Position: Striker
Date of birth: 26/11/1991
Previous clubs: Atalanta, Cittadella, Juventus, Bologna, Sampdoria, Napoli
Joined Saints: 2017
Height: 181cm
Weight: 72kg
Nationality: Italian

PROFILE: Italian striker Gabbiadini arrived at St Mary's in the January 2017 transfer window from Napoli. With the ability to play in a number of attacking positions, Gabbiadini provides Saints with excellent options going forward. With a real eye for goal and a powerful left foot, the Italian showed his qualities right from the off at Saints, scoring in each of his first four matches.

2016/17 KEY STATS: 12 games played, six goals scored, 2 Wembley goals

2016/17 STANDOUT MOMENT: Having made a remarkable impact in his first two games, Gabbiadini showed his excellence in front of goal once again in the EFL Cup final at Wembley. After having a strike incorrectly ruled out for offside, the Italian hit back with a close-range finish and then a stunning left-footed half-volley to draw Saints level. Despite being on the losing side, many saw Gabbiadini as the man of the match.

PLAYER PROFILES

21 RYAN BERTRAND

Position: Defender
Date of birth: 05/08/1989
Previous clubs: Chelsea, Bournemouth, Oldham Athletic, Norwich City, Reading, Nottingham Forest, Aston Villa
Joined Saints: 2014
Height: 179cm
Weight: 85kg
Nationality: English

PROFILE: An attacking full-back for both Southampton and England, Bertrand has gone from strength to strength since his arrival at St Mary's from Chelsea in 2014. With the confidence and ability to play centre-back, left-back or wing-back, Bertrand possesses plenty of defensive qualities. But he is also excellent going forward, providing a great outlet down the left-hand side for Saints when attacking, chipping in with some important goals and assists.

2016/17 KEY STATS: 34 games played, 3 goals, 4 assists

2016/17 STANDOUT MOMENT: Having netted in Saints' EFL Cup win at Arsenal a few weeks previously, Bertrand scored another important goal in the 3-1 win at AFC Bournemouth. Losing by a single goal heading towards half time, the left-back did superbly well to create space in the penalty area, before firing a low shot into the far corner. It was a superb finish, and helped Saints on their way to a big three points.

22 NATHAN REDMOND

Position: Midfielder
Date of birth: 06/03/1994
Previous clubs: Birmingham City, Norwich City
Joined Saints: 2016
Height: 173cm
Weight: 69kg
Nationality: English

PROFILE: Arriving at St Mary's with a reputation as a goalscoring winger, Redmond spent much of his early Saints career playing as a striker. Possessing plenty of pace and skill, as well as a direct style of play, Redmond is a real handful for opposing defenders. He showed his eye for goal throughout his first season with Saints, netting eight times, as well as making his debut for the England senior team.

2016/17 KEY STATS: 50 games played, 8 goals scored, 76 chances created

2016/17 STANDOUT MOMENT: While Redmond's senior England debut was a special moment for the youngster, his goal against Liverpool in the EFL Cup semi-final first leg must go down as the best moment from his first full campaign with Southampton. The winger collected Jay Rodriguez's pass before firing it in superbly, to give Saints a vital first-leg advantage.

23 PIERRE-EMILE HØJBJERG

Position: Midfielder
Date of birth: 05/08/1995
Previous clubs: Bayern Munich, Schalke 04, FC Augsburg
Joined Saints: 2016
Height: 1185cm
Weight: 85kg
Nationality: Danish

PROFILE: Midfielder Højbjerg arrived in the summer of 2016 from German giants Bayern Munich. Despite his young age, the Danish international showed plenty of maturity and experience on and off the pitch for Saints during his first season in England. With an excellent range of passing and tremendous workrate, Højbjerg has the potential to be a key player for many years to come.

2016/17 KEY STATS: 35 games played, 87% pass completion, 23 chances created

2016/17 STANDOUT MOMENT: Having arrived from German side Bayern Munich, Højbjerg quickly set about making an impression in English football. He did just that, earning Southampton's Under Armour August Player of the Month award for his performances during the opening month of the campaign.

PLAYER PROFILES

25 FLORIN GARDOS

Position: Defender
Date of birth: 29/10/1988
Previous clubs: Concordia Chiajna, Steaua Bucuresti
Joined Saints: 2014
Height: 193cm
Weight: 84kg
Nationality: Romanian

PROFILE: The defender has been extremely unfortunate with injuries since joining Saints in 2014. After making 11 appearances in his first season, the Romanian international missed the entire 2015/16 campaign through injury, regaining full fitness midway through the 2016/17 season. When fully fit, Gardos is a commanding presence defensively, with good technical ability.

2016/17 KEY STATS: 1 game played, 1 interception, 1 clearance

2016/17 STANDOUT MOMENT: Gardos's season was once again hampered by injury, but he will have taken a lot of pride from his comeback game in the Emirates FA Cup clash with Arsenal. While Saints may have lost the match, Gardos came through the 90 minutes unscathed – his only first-team appearance of a difficult campaign for the Romanian.

26 JÉRÉMY PIED

Position: Defender
Date of birth: 23/02/1989
Previous clubs: Lyon, Metz, Nice, Guingamp
Joined Saints: 2016
Height: 173cm
Weight: 69kg
Nationality: French

PROFILE: With plenty of attacking threat, much of Pied's early career was spent as a right-winger. As his career developed in France, he also showed potential at right-back. Pied's pace means he provides an option for Saints in attacking positions, but the Frenchman also has excellent defensive qualities. A long-term knee injury meant his first season with Saints was limited to just four matches.

2016/17 KEY STATS: 4 games played, 66% tackle win ratio, 1 chance created

2016/17 STANDOUT MOMENT: The right-back's first full game back from injury will have been a hugely important milestone for the Frenchman. Having picked up the injury so early into his career with Saints, coming back into the side and helping the team beat Middlesbrough will have tasted that little bit sweeter for Pied. Many supporters praised the right-back for his performance in that game.

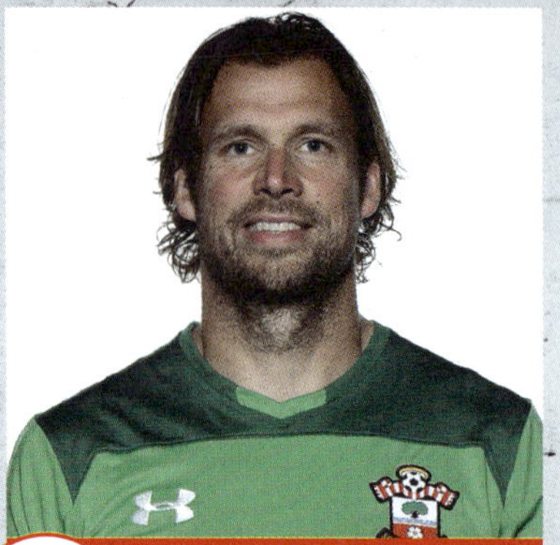

28 STUART TAYLOR

Position: Goalkeeper
Date of birth: 28/11/1980
Previous clubs: Arsenal, Bristol Rovers, Crystal Palace, Peterborough United, Leicester City, Aston Villa, Cardiff City, Manchester City, Reading, Yeovil Town, Leeds United
Joined Saints: 2016
Height: 196cm
Weight: 85kg
Nationality: English

PROFILE: Having started his career with Arsenal, Taylor has spent much of his time since as a back-up goalkeeper, playing for clubs including Aston Villa, Manchester City and Leeds United. Taylor joined Saints as back-up to Fraser Forster and Alex McCarthy, providing experience and knowledge to the two England goalkeepers.

2016/17 STANDOUT MOMENT: After Fraser Forster's penalty save in the 0-0 draw against Liverpool at Anfield, the goalkeeper was full of praise for Taylor's contribution. The two had previously discussed ways to put off penalty taker James Milner, and it worked brilliantly, with Forster denying the left-back and earning Saints a point.

PLAYER PROFILES

30 WILL WOOD

Position: Defender
Date of birth: 29/11/1996
Previous clubs:
Southampton Academy
Joined Saints: 2009
Height: 183cm
Weight: 80kg
Nationality: English

PROFILE: Capable of playing at both centre-back and left-back, Wood's versatility has helped him progress through Southampton's Academy since the age of 12. The defender made an impressive step-up to Under-21 level during the 2014/15 campaign, and he has continued to show his qualities since then, becoming a key figure in Martin Hunter's Under-23 side.

2016/17 KEY STATS:
14 appearances for Southampton's Under-23s side.

2016/17 STANDOUT MOMENT:
After missing much of the 2015/16 campaign through injury, the defender will have been delighted to get back to full fitness and make his mark again. He impressed for the Under-23s after returning in late November.

32 ALFIE JONES

Position: Defender
Date of birth: 07/10/1997
Previous clubs:
Southampton Academy
Joined Saints: 2007
Height: 187cm
Weight: 77kg
Nationality: English

PROFILE: With a calm and composed nature, Jones is confident at both centre-back and in a defensive midfield role. The youngster has been a key figure for Southampton's Under-23s in recent seasons, with his impressive performances catching the eye of first-team staff. The youngster was named as the club's Young Player of the Year in 2016.

2016/17 KEY STATS:
31 appearances, four goals and one assist for Southampton's Under-23 side.

2016/17 STANDOUT MOMENT:
Jones's form for the Under-23 side was picked up on by first-team coaching staff, with the youngster often stepping up to the senior side for training sessions. He will hope a first-team debut is not too far away now, as he looks to continue his excellent progress.

33 MATT TARGETT

Position: Defender
Date of birth: 18/09/1995
Previous clubs:
Southampton Academy
Joined Saints: 2003
Height: 183cm
Weight: 70kg
Nationality: English

PROFILE: Spotted at one of Saints Foundation's soccer schools when he was eight, Targett has worked his way through the club's famed Academy. With an excellent left-foot, Targett has mainly featured as a left-back throughout his career so far, but can also play further forward down the left. Targett has represented England at Under-21 level on a regular basis over the last two years.

2016/17 KEY STATS: 8 games played, 10 chances created, 80% tackle win ratio

2016/17 STANDOUT MOMENT:
Having picked up a long-term injury after a positive start to the campaign, in which he made seven appearances in all competitions, Targett will have taken plenty of satisfaction from his return to action in the penultimate match of the season, against Manchester United at St Mary's.

PLAYER PROFILES

34 JAKE FLANNIGAN

Position: Midfielder
Date of birth: 02/02/1996
Previous clubs:
Southampton Academy
Joined Saints: 2003
Height: 172cm
Weight: 77kg
Nationality: English

PROFILE: A serious knee injury shortly after featuring on the first-team bench back in February 2015 halted Flannigan's progress. The youngster, who can play at right-back or in midfield, made his comeback in November 2016, and signed a new one-year contract extension ahead of the 2017/18 campaign. He featured for the first-team during pre-season.

2016/17 KEY STATS: Three appearances and one assist for Southampton's Under-23s side.

2016/17 STANDOUT MOMENT: After two serious knee injuries kept Flannigan out of action for almost two years, the versatile youngster was thrilled to make his comeback in Southampton Under-23s' 1-0 away win against Swansea City in November 2016.

38 SAM MCQUEEN

Position: Defender
Date of birth: 06/02/1995
Previous clubs:
Southampton Academy,
Southend United
Joined Saints: 2003
Height: 181cm
Weight: 70kg
Nationality: English

PROFILE: McQueen spent much of his youth career playing as a left-winger, featuring there for Saints' Academy sides and Southend United during a successful loan spell. But during the 2016/17 campaign, McQueen showed his qualities as a left-back, featuring regularly in the absence of Ryan Bertrand and Matt Targett. McQueen's performances received plenty of praise throughout the season, as he adapted superbly to his new role.

2016/17 KEY STATS: 20 games played, 5 chances created, 24 crosses

2016/17 STANDOUT MOMENT: Having come on for the injured Matt Targett against Burnley in a Premier League match, four days later McQueen made his first start for Saints – against Internazionale in the San Siro. The youngster put in a mature and confident performance, with Saints unfortunate not to come away with something from the game against the Italian giants.

39 JOSH SIMS

Position: Midfielder
Date of birth: 28/03/1997
Previous clubs:
Southampton Academy
Joined Saints: 2011
Height: 168cm
Weight: 67kg
Nationality: English

PROFILE: With plenty of pace and trickery, Sims proves a real handful for any defender he comes up against. The winger made his Premier League debut during the 2016/17 season, helping Saints to a 1-0 win against Everton. He also set up Shane Long's decisive goal in the EFL Cup semi-final second leg thanks to his pace and direct approach. The youngster has represented England at Under-17, Under-18 and Under-20 level.

2016/17 KEY STATS: 13 games played, 2 assists, 6 Premier League 2 goals

2016/17 STANDOUT MOMENT: While Sims' EFL Cup semi-final assist comes close, his incredible performance on his debut against Everton has to be the youngster's top moment. Sims set up Charlie Austin for the opening goal inside a minute and continued to cause problems for Ronald Koeman's side throughout the game. Saints won 1-0, and Sims was named Man of the Match.

PLAYER PROFILES

42 JAKE HESKETH

Position: Midfielder
Date of birth: 27/03/1996
Previous clubs: Southampton Academy
Joined Saints: 2006
Height: 168cm
Weight: 63kg
Nationality: English

PROFILE: A product of Southampton's famed youth academy, Hesketh is an attacking midfielder who looks to bridge the gap between midfield and attack. The youngster loves to find pockets of space and play clever passes through to the strikers. Hesketh can also play on either wing, but it is in the number ten role where he thrives and looks the most dangerous.

2016/17 KEY STATS: 2 games played, 1 goal, 79% pass completion

2016/17 STANDOUT MOMENT: Handed his first senior start in almost two years, Hesketh made the most of his opportunity, netting his first professional goal in Saints' 2-0 EFL Cup win against Crystal Palace at St Mary's. The youngster celebrated with fellow Academy graduates Matt Targett, James Ward-Prowse and Harrison Reed, in what was a very iconic moment for everyone at the club.

43 YAN VALERY

Position: Defender
Date of birth: 22/02/1999
Previous clubs: Stade Rennais
Joined Saints: 2015
Height: 183cm
Weight: 79kg
Nationality: French

PROFILE: A French youth international, Valery joined Southampton from Stade Rennais in 2015, initially playing for the club's Under-18s. His impressive performances saw him step up to the Under-23 squad and continue to make his mark. An attacking full-back, Valery signed his first professional deal in 2016, and has represented the first team in pre-season friendlies.

2016/17 KEY STATS: 21 appearances and one assist for Southampton's Under-23s side. Eight appearances and one goal for the Under-18s.

2016/17 STANDOUT MOMENT: The defender received international recognition with France Under-18s in March. The call-up came just a few days after Valery had netted a goal in Saints Under-18s' 2-0 win against Brighton & Hove Albion. Not a bad week for the youngster!

44 FRASER FORSTER

Position: Goalkeeper
Date of birth: 17/03/1988
Previous clubs: Newcastle United, Bristol Rovers, Norwich City, Stockport County, Celtic
Joined Saints: 2014
Height: 201cm
Weight: 93kg
Nationality: English

PROFILE: An England international, Forster has come to the rescue on a number of occasions for Saints since his move from Scottish side Celtic in 2014. At 6ft 7in, the stopper is a commanding presence in goal, and has made a number of crucial saves during his time at St Mary's. His record-breaking 708 minutes without conceding during the 2015/16 season will take some beating for years to come.

2016/17 KEY STATS: 48 games played, 19 clean sheets, 98 saves made

2016/17 STANDOUT MOMENT: Forster's best moment came at Anfield in the second leg of the EFL Cup semi-final. With Saints leading 1-0 on aggregate, the stopper couldn't hold on to Emre Can's shot and it looked as though Liverpool would equalise. But Forster had other ideas, turning quickly and somehow scooping the ball off the line and away to safety. Everyone remembers what happened next!

SPOT THE DIFFERENCE

HERE'S A GREAT SHOT OF JAMES WARD-PROWSE CELEBRATING HIS GOAL AGAINST WEST HAM UNITED. BUT CAN YOU SPOT THE FIVE DIFFERENCES BETWEEN THE TWO PHOTOS?

ANSWERS:

1

2

3

4

5

THE SAINTS STORE

THERE ARE SO MANY GREAT PRODUCTS AVAILABLE TO BUY FROM OUR SAINTS STORES! WE'VE PICKED OUT TEN GREAT ITEMS HERE THAT YOU CAN GET YOUR HANDS ON AT OUR STADIUM OR WESTQUAY STORES, AS WELL AS ONLINE AT STORE.SAINTSFC.CO.UK...

Street Football (Size 4)
£12

Dinosaur Soft Toy
£14

Sekonda Black Watch
£30

Mascot Backpack
£20

Plush Piggybank
£9

Large Stationery Set
£12

Youth Home Shirt
£40

Kit Wheeled Backpack
£30

Youth Away Shirt
£40

Reversible Home/Away Scarf
£12

STORE.SAINTSFC.CO.UK

GOALKEEPING TIPS

WITH VINCE BARTRAM

SOUTHAMPTON'S ACADEMY GOALKEEPING MANAGER VINCE BARTRAM TELLS US WHAT YOUNG KEEPERS NEED TO BE SUCCESSFUL.

WHAT ARE THE CORE SKILLS YOU LOOK FOR?

We look for good athletes first and foremost. Movement skill is a big thing – speed around the goal – especially as the Premier League is so quick now, so we look for the potential to move well. We don't expect them to be lightning quick straight away, as it's stuff we can develop with footwork drills, but they need to be athletes first and foremost.

The actual skill sets as a goalkeeper? Again we're looking for potential, so things like good, clean hands, distribution and movement. If the ball is two yards away from you, you can't catch it without moving your feet. Everyone thinks the hands are the most important part of a goalkeeper, but for me it's actually the feet, because that's what gets your body into position to catch the ball.

IS THERE ANY ADVICE YOU CAN GIVE TO YOUNG KEEPERS FOR TRAINING OR DURING GAMES?

As keepers, we talk being on your toes in a set position. It's very simple, but very effective. What you need to do is bend your knees so you can't see your toes and then lean forward slightly so you can see your toes again. Invariably, that lifts your heels off the floor!

For a goalkeeper, in most of your movements your heel shouldn't be touching the floor. We're working on our toes with our weight slightly forward, our chest just in front of our knees and head in front of our toes – that then helps you be light and quick on your feet, and nicely balanced, and then your head can lead all the movements from there.

HOW IMPORTANT IS COMMUNICATION AS A KEEPER?

It's massive. I always tell my keepers to talk their way through the game. If they don't

have to touch the ball but they've done all the talking and communicating to get the defence to do the job for them then that's the ideal way to keep a clean sheet, so keep talking!

HOW ABOUT DISTRIBUTION AND HANDLING?

It's the basics – make your game simple and keep it simple. The game is quicker, they design boots to purposely swerve the ball, they design the balls to move in the air and be quicker through it, so it gives us a problem. If you can be quick on your feet and make the catch easier for yourself and make it simple by having good, fundamental techniques you're giving yourself an advantage.

There is then an adaptability that comes in – the blocking saves, coming out and smothering and spreading – but you still need the basic skills of catching a ball and passing a ball.

We have six team targets that we debrief after each game, and all of those areas our goalkeepers can effect. One of them is switching play, so if you receive a ball from the right-back, most of the players will be on that side of the pitch, so the space is to the left side. So if you can switch the play it means the player who receives the ball from you should have more space, so in theory you're making it easier for your team to build an attack.

DRILLS

HERE ARE A SELECTION OF KEEPER DRILLS YOU CAN DO AT HOME.

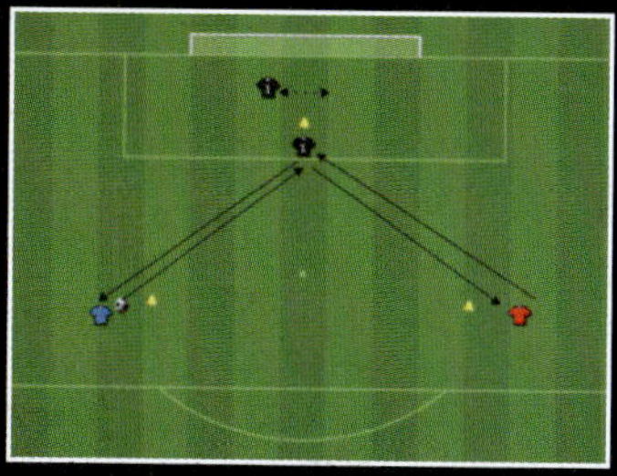

1. Goalkeeper stands inside the cones. The blue shirt passes the ball to the goalkeeper's left foot. The keeper then plays the ball with his right foot to the red shirt (repeat ten times, then reverse).

2. Goalkeeper stands behind the cone. The blue shirt passes to the goalkeeper, who takes two touches to play around the back of the cone and pass to the red shirt. Red then passes back to the keeper to repeat back to blue (repeat ten times – then another ten times with the keeper choosing either one or two touch).

3. Goalkeeper stands behind the cone. Blue shirt plays ball across the front of the cone. Goalkeeper plays one-touch pass to red shirt (then reverse and repeat ten times).

4. Goalkeeper stands behind the cone. Blue shirt chooses to play across the front of the cone for a one-touch pass, or behind the cone for a two-touch pass to red (repeat in reverse and repeat ten times).

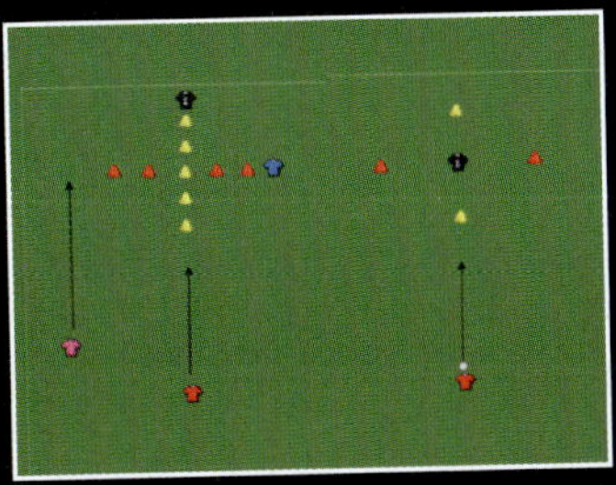

1. Goalkeeper moves down the centre line of yellow cones to receive the ball from the red shirt (repeat four times).

2. Goalkeeper (blue) moves across the central line of red cones to receive the ball from the pink shirt (repeat four times).

3. Goalkeeper stands in middle of the diamond, then moves around each cone and back to the middle for service from the red shirt.

4. Goalkeeper stands in the middle of the diamond and moves to each cone and back to the middle for service from the red shirt.

5. As 3, but double cones.

6. As 4, but double cones.

KIT ROOM SECRETS

MARK FORBES HAS BEEN SOUTHAMPTON'S KIT & EQUIPMENT MANAGER FOR THE PAST EIGHT YEARS. HERE, HE TELLS US THE SECRETS OF BEING THE CLUB'S KIT MAN!

WHAT IS THE BUILD-UP TO A MATCH LIKE FOR YOU?

I have a very good team. I'm very well supported by Jamie Ireland, who is my assistant, David Price as the Academy kit officer, Ben Hartnell-Parker, Denise Bullock and Frankie, my wife, who also works for the club.

To summarise what we do: We have to make sure we've got the right kit and the right equipment in the right place, for the right team, at the right time!

When we're talking about a match day, it's important we remember it's across the entire group of players – that's from the Under-7s through to the First Team. So we are preparing 16 or 17 teams for match day.

We're getting everything ready – match kit, boots, medical kit and equipment. Our job is to make sure everything is collated and ready.

HOW MUCH OF A CHALLENGE IS TRANSPORTING ALL THE KIT AND EQUIPMENT?

It's exciting and challenging, probably in equal measure. We don't keep anything at the stadium – our home is Staplewood. We only use the stadium on a match day.

Home games aren't as bad, because we start to transport kit and equipment over on a Thursday for a Saturday game. Typically, you're looking after about 20 players in the squad and about 14 or 15 support staff, including the senior management coaching team.

The last thing always to go over will be the football boots and shinpads, because the squad tends not to be announced until after training on the morning prior to the game.

Away games are more challenging. First of all, you've got to get there. If we're playing a game long distance, the team tend to fly. I will go ahead of the team in the Black Pearl – that's the name for our kit van! – which will be filled with just about everything, except the boots. Meanwhile Jamie is back at the training ground, with David and Ben, and he will make sure the boots get packed, then he will fly up with the team and one flight skip containing the boots. Jamie and I then go down to the ground the night before and set everything up.

Some dressing rooms, particularly at newer stadiums, are fantastic – the Etihad, at Manchester City for example, Arsenal, Tottenham, Liverpool are really good. Some of the older stadiums are more of a challenge. So Crystal Palace is a very small dressing room, and logistically that's very challenging. The same at Stoke. But kit men get to know each other and there's a support network. We all make sure we have what each other needs.

WHAT'S A MATCH DAY LIKE FOR YOU?

For a 3pm game, we go to the ground at about 9.30am. It

takes us approximately two-and-a-half hours to finish setting up, so we're finished about midday. We have about an hour when we can grab a cup of tea and a sandwich, because from the moment the team arrives it's our job to make sure everything they need or want is accounted for.

It's a long day, but a very exciting one. It's the best day in the calendar, and when you win it's the best feeling in the world, and when you lose it's the worst feeling.

WHAT'S THE STRANGEST THING A PLAYER HAS ASKED FOR?

Typically, it will be spare underpants, a certain type of toothpaste, toothbrush, hair gel, deodorant. I can think of one player who likes to wear a lucky band and I needed to get them a red band. I can think of another who wants to cut socks in a different way. We have one player who has a superstition where his shirt mustn't be hung up. We've got a few who maybe want a certain type of energy drink chilled and put in a certain spot. Some want kit put in a certain way.

Every one of them probably has some little routine and it's fair to say we will always try to accommodate it, because, if it puts them in a happy frame of mind, hopefully at the end of the day we've got the result.

HAVE YOU EVER FORGOTTEN SOMETHING?

This is my eighth season and collectively among us I can think of probably four occasions where we've maybe made a minor mistake – one occasion where we left one pair of boots behind – but it's few and far between, thankfully!

WHAT'S THE BEST THING ABOUT BEING SOUTHAMPTON'S KITMAN?

I've been supporting Saints for 54 years and my mum will still embarrass me in front of people, because I've still got a little book from when I was five that says 'One day I will work for Southampton Football Club,' so I guess my dream's come true. Just to be part of it is a tremendous privilege.

WHAT'S THE TOUGHEST THING?

Defeat! But, although that's the worst feeling, when we win it's the best feeling, and you can see it on the fans' faces.

Also, I go everywhere in the Black Pearl, and I have to say roadworks! You're coming back from Newcastle late at night and you've suddenly got to do a two-hour diversion at Newbury – that's not fun!

IN NUMBERS: SOUTHAMPTON'S KIT DEPARTMENT

32500
New items of kit to be sorted out for the season

500
Pairs of boots handled during the season for the First Team

300
Towels washed EVERY day

200
Kits that can be washed on a single day

400
Kits that can be washed on a single day when the weather's bad!

400
Packs of chewing gum bought per season for the players

STRENGTHEN YOUR GAME

WE SPOKE WITH TOM HENSON, SOUTHAMPTON'S LEAD ACADEMY STRENGTH & CONDITIONING COACH, to find out about the importance of strength and conditioning for the Saints players and to get some tips to improve your own game...

HOW IMPORTANT IS STRENGTH & CONDITIONING IN THE MODERN GAME?

The game has changed massively compared to decades gone by. The overall distance you cover in a match is more or less the same, but the intensity has gone up massively – the amount of high-speed running, sprint distance, jumps and power actions have massively increased.

So players these days need to be able to cover the same distance and have the same aerobic base as players that played in the 1980s or 1990s, but at this point we need to be able to produce much more force and much more speed and repeat that throughout the match.

Strength and conditioning really provides a physiological underpinning for that. It provides you with the basis to be able to produce those forceful and high-intensity actions.

HOW MUCH OF A FOCUS IS THERE ON STRENGTH & CONDITIONING IN THE SOUTHAMPTON ACADEMY?

We have a huge emphasis on it, and what we do with the Academy and what we do with the first team are kind of a continuation of each other.

But, with young players, the focus is a lot more on movement, and a bit less on load. The older age group is more focused on load, speed and force production.

As you're growing up, your body is going through a lot of changes and, for us, it's about making your brain better able to coordinate and integrate movement, rather than necessarily load it to be able to produce as much force as possible. That comes as you get older.

HOW MUCH OF A DIFFERENCE DOES IT MAKE FOR YOUNGER PLAYERS AS THEY PROGRESS?

In general, a player with better movement competency, stronger muscles and joints, and somebody who has been loaded repeatedly throughout their life will be more injury-proof.

Their ability to produce force means they are less at risk when producing force in a match. So, if you have somebody who hasn't been strength trained and they look to produce maximum force within a game, the risk of muscle damage is huge.

But if you look at players like Josh Sims, Jake Hesketh and Harrison Reed – ones who have all come through to the first team – they would have all followed a very similar plan as they moved through the Academy, and all of those boys move well, have great top speeds, can jump high and are in general very injury-proof.

If you watched Simsy against, say, Liverpool last year, some of the tackles that he rides show how he's so good at controlling his body. His centre of gravity is so low. He just knows how to control his own movement, and then obviously he's got that crazy top speed, which set up Shane Long to get us to Wembley. That sort of thing is born out of great football understanding, but also strength and conditioning.

ANY TIPS FOR KIDS OUTSIDE OF OUR ACADEMY TO IMPROVE?

If they're not in the Southampton set-up, what we encourage kids to do is play different sports.

Football will put your body in similar positions all the time, and sometimes to learn optimal movements or to train your body effectively in all sorts of different movements, you're going to have to get outside of football and do something different.

We'd encourage you to learn about some of the simple gym movements that you can do at home – press ups, squats, split squats – but also to just go and look at playing different sports that move you in a different way. Climb on things, jump on things – just learn how to move your body differently outside of football, because if you're into it you'll naturally get a lot of time playing football.

Even within the Southampton set-up, we've got a big multi-sport culture, where we try to play as many variations of different sports that we can, just to make sure the boys aren't overusing their bodies, but are also stimulating different movement pathways and understanding of their bodies.

If you're a slightly older age group, you can look at strengthening slightly. We'd probably look to integrate some basic, fundamental compound movements that will help to develop strength and you can do those with just body weight at those age groups – press-ups, squats, pull-ups and then some sort of core movement would make a great programme to put in alongside football sessions. It would really help with developing speed and injury prevention.

Kids should be playing different sports, not just football, with the aim of it improving your football.

If you were without a coach and didn't have the same set-up we have here, good advice would be to do some basic strength work, some repeated speed that you're comfortable with, some jumping, some landing, then play as many different sports as you can and just enjoy your football training.

PREMIER LEAGUE FOCUS

AFC BOURNEMOUTH

NICKNAME: THE CHERRIES
FOUNDED: 1899
GROUND: VITALITY STADIUM
CAPACITY: 11,464
LAST SEASON: 9TH

KEY MAN: JOSHUA KING

The Norway international scored 16 Premier League goals in 36 appearances during the 2016/17 campaign, helping the Cherries record their highest ever finish in the top flight of English football.

ARSENAL

NICKNAME: THE GUNNERS
FOUNDED: 1886
GROUND: EMIRATES STADIUM
CAPACITY: 60,432
LAST SEASON: 5TH

KEY MAN: ALEXANDRE LACAZETTE

The France international striker joined the Gunners in the summer for a club-record fee from Lyon, where he averaged a goal almost every two games. Arsenal will hope he brings them similar firepower.

BRIGHTON & HOVE ALBION

NICKNAME: THE SEAGULLS
FOUNDED: 1901
GROUND: AMERICAN EXPRESS COMMUNITY STADIUM
CAPACITY: 30,750
LAST SEASON: 2ND (CHAMPIONSHIP)

KEY MAN: ANTHONY KNOCKAERT

A key factor in Brighton's promotion from the Championship, Knockaert was named as the Football League Player of the Season for his efforts during 2016/17. The winger netted 13 goals in 39 appearances.

BURNLEY

NICKNAME: THE CLARETS
FOUNDED: 1882
GROUND: TURF MOOR
CAPACITY: 21,800
LAST SEASON: 16TH

KEY MAN: TOM HEATON

The goalkeeper's form during the 2016/17 season was rewarded with a first England start in June. Heaton made 36 appearances in all competitions, keeping ten clean sheets as Burnley survived in the Premier League.

CHELSEA

NICKNAME: THE BLUES
FOUNDED: 1905
GROUND: STAMFORD BRIDGE
CAPACITY: 41,631
LAST SEASON: 1ST

KEY MAN: N'GOLO KANTÉ

Aiming to win the Premier League for a third season in a row, the 2016/17 PFA Players' Player of the Year is hugely important for Chelsea. His constant energy means he is a real asset both going forward and defensively.

CRYSTAL PALACE

NICKNAME: THE EAGLES
FOUNDED: 1905
GROUND: SELHURST PARK
CAPACITY: 25,456
LAST SEASON: 14TH

KEY MAN: WILFRIED ZAHA

The winger signed a new five-year contract ahead of the 2017/18 campaign. Zaha, an Ivory Coast international, has plenty of tricks up his sleeve to torment defenders, netting seven goals and grabbing 11 assists last season.

EVERTON

NICKNAME: THE TOFFEES
FOUNDED: 1878
GROUND: GOODISON PARK
CAPACITY: 39,572
LAST SEASON: 7TH

KEY MAN: MORGAN SCHNEIDERLIN

Former Southampton midfielder Schneiderlin joined Everton in January 2017, making an immediate impact. His composure on the ball and range of passing are vital for Ronald Koeman's Toffees to play at their best.

HUDDERSFIELD TOWN

NICKNAME: THE TERRIES
FOUNDED: 1908
GROUND: JOHN SMITH'S STADIUM
CAPACITY: 24,500
LAST SEASON: 5TH (CHAMPIONSHIP)

KEY MAN: AARON MOOY

Sensational in midfield for the Terriers as they won promotion, and made his loan switch from Manchester City permanent in the summer. If he can have a similar impact in the top-flight, Huddersfield's survival hopes will be significantly boosted.

LEICESTER CITY

NICKNAME: THE FOXES
FOUNDED: 1884
GROUND: KING POWER STADIUM
CAPACITY: 32,315
LAST SEASON: 12TH

KEY MAN: JAMIE VARDY

While his form may not have matched that from the 2015/16 campaign, Vardy's goals are vital for the Foxes. He scored 16 times in all competitions during 2016/17, including two in the UEFA Champions League.

LIVERPOOL

NICKNAME: THE REDS
FOUNDED: 1892
GROUND: ANFIELD
CAPACITY: 54,074
LAST SEASON: 4TH

KEY MAN: SADIO MANÉ

Former Southampton winger Mané was excellent during his first season at Anfield, with his pace and trickery causing plenty of problems. He netted 13 times in the Premier League before injury ended his season early.

MANCHESTER CITY

NICKNAME: THE CITIZENS
FOUNDED: 1894
GROUND: ETIHAD STADIUM
CAPACITY: 55,097
LAST SEASON: 3RD

KEY MAN: GABRIEL JESUS

He only arrived in January 2017, but Brazilian forward Jesus made quite an impact for City. Netting six goals in ten games, he'll be one to watch out for as he develops under manager Pep Guardiola at the Etihad Stadium.

MANCHESTER UNITED

NICKNAME: THE RED DEVILS
FOUNDED: 1878
GROUND: OLD TRAFFORD
CAPACITY: 75,643
LAST SEASON: 6TH

KEY MAN: PAUL POGBA

A world-record signing in 2016, Pogba netted the opening goal in Manchester United's Europa League success last season. The midfielder will now be hoping to kick on during his second full campaign back at Old Trafford.

NEWCASTLE UNITED

NICKNAME: THE MAPGIES
FOUNDED: 1892
GROUND: ST JAMES' PARK
CAPACITY: 52,354
LAST SEASON: 1ST (CHAMPIONSHIP)

KEY MAN: MATT RITCHIE

Having shown his quality in the Premier League already with Bournemouth, winger Ritchie will hope to pick up where he left off with Newcastle. The Scottish international netted 16 goals in all competitions during 2016/17.

STOKE CITY

NICKNAME: THE POTTERS
FOUNDED: 1863
GROUND: BET365 STADIUM
CAPACITY: 27,902
LAST SEASON: 13TH

KEY MAN: JOE ALLEN

Having arrived at the bet365 Stadium with a reputation as a solid defensive midfielder, Welshman Allen showed his quality going forward during his first season with the Potters, netting six goals in the Premier League.

SWANSEA CITY

NICKNAME: THE SWANS
FOUNDED: 1912
GROUND: LIBERTY STADIUM
CAPACITY: 21,088
LAST SEASON: 15TH

KEY MAN: WILFRIED BONY

A hero for the Swans before a big money move to Manchester City in 2015, the powerful striker is now back at the club, after re-joining on transfer deadline day.

TOTTENHAM HOTSPUR

NICKNAME: SPURS
FOUNDED: 1882
GROUND: WEMBLEY
CAPACITY: 90,000
LAST SEASON: 2ND

KEY MAN: HARRY KANE

With a number of exciting young players, Kane is without doubt the most important. The England international netted 35 goals in total during 2016/17, winning the Premier League Golden Boot for the second season in a row.

WATFORD

NICKNAME: THE HORNETS
FOUNDED: 1881
GROUND: VICARAGE ROAD
CAPACITY: 21,438
LAST SEASON: 17TH

KEY MAN: TROY DEENEY

The forward causes plenty of problems for defences with his power and direct style of play. The Watford captain netted ten goals in all competitions during the 2016/17 campaign, helping the Hornets avoid relegation.

WEST BROMWICH ALBION

NICKNAME: THE BAGGIES
FOUNDED: 1878
GROUND: THE HAWTHORNS
CAPACITY: 26,852
LAST SEASON: 10TH

KEY MAN: BEN FOSTER

An ever-present for the Baggies during the 2016/17 campaign, Foster made a number of excellent stops to help West Brom to a top ten Premier League finish. The English stopper kept six clean sheets in total last season.

WEST HAM UNITED

NICKNAME: THE HAMMERS
FOUNDED: 1895
GROUND: LONDON STADIUM
CAPACITY: 60,000
LAST SEASON: 11TH

KEY MAN: MICHAIL ANTONIO

The powerful winger, who signed a new contract on the back of his excellent form in 2016/17, scored nine Premier League goals and grabbed five assists last season, as well as earning international recognition with England.

QUIZ ANSWERS

QUIZ OF THE SEASON (P22)

1. Fraser Forster
2. Nathan Redmond (1-1 vs Watford)
3. Dušan Tadić (Five)
4. Shane Long (28 in all competitions)
5. Josh Sims
6. Virgil van Dijk and Charlie Austin (Two)
7. James Ward-Prowse (3-0 vs Leicester City)
8. Jack Stephens and Oriol Romeu
9. Four (Two in the EFL Cup, two in the Premier League)
10. Six (One vs West Ham, two vs Sunderland, two vs Manchester United, one vs Watford)
11. Sofiane Boufal
12. Ten (James Ward-Prowse, Harrison Reed, Jack Stephens, Lloyd Isgrove, Olufela Olomola, Matt Targett, Sam McQueen, Josh Sims, Harry Lewis, Jake Hesketh)
13. Maya Yoshida
14. Jordy Clasie
15. Jay Rodriguez (H vs Sunderland (league) and A vs Middlesbrough (league)) and Sofiane Boufal (H vs Sunderland (EFL Cup) and H vs Middlesbrough (league))
16. 2003 (FA Cup final vs Arsenal)
17. 13
18. Oriol Romeu and Ryan Bertrand
19. Steven Davis (Virgil van Dijk was named Team Captain)
20. Five (Crystal Palace, Sunderland, Arsenal, Liverpool (H), Liverpool (A))

WORDSEARCH (P29)

R	I	W	S	M	H	G	D	F	W	R	Y	H
E	R	N	M	T	L	N	M	N	D	N	T	E
T	U	J	I	Z	A	K	H	L	K	N	D	R
S	O	N	Y	D	B	P	L	V	I	Q	B	O
R	M	N	L	T	A	R	L	A	C	O	D	E
O	R	Q	P	E	W	I	S	E	U	X	B	S
F	A	H	H	H	T	Y	B	F	W	P	L	Y
N	R	L	Y	F	M	I	A	B	T	O	M	K
W	E	K	T	M	D	L	S	Z	A	E	O	M
K	D	H	A	B	V	K	R	S	D	G	K	D
H	N	S	M	G	O	A	L	A	I	N	M	M
K	U	R	O	M	E	U	C	G	X	E	N	R
B	G	L	E	U	G	A	E	L	L	N	R	X

QUIZ ANSWERS

HIDDEN WORD (P29)

1. REDMOND
2. DAVIS
3. GABBIADINI
4. EIGHTH
5. FORSTER
6. ROMEU
7. LIVERPOOL
8. HESKETH
9. TERRYPAINE
10. UNDERARMOUR
11. STOKES
12. THEDELL
13. SIMS

Key Answer =
MADE FOR HEROES

SPOT THE DIFFERENCE (P48)

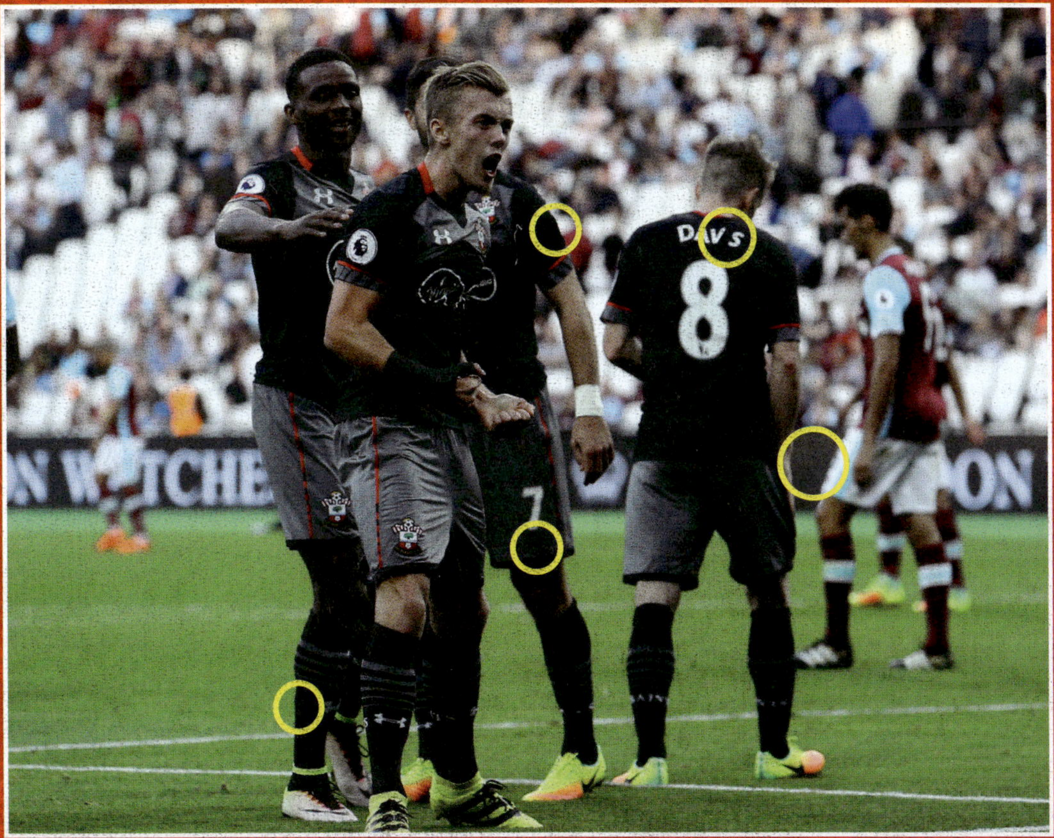

SPOT THE SAINTS

WE'VE HIDDEN A HOST OF SOUTHAMPTON STARS IN THIS PHOTO! CAN YOU FIND MAURICIO PELLEGRINO, MANOLO GABBIADINI, NATHAN REDMOND, PIERRE-EMILE HØJBJERG AND STUART TAYLOR?

INDIAN COOKING

Designed by Sally Strugnell and Claire Leighton
Illustrations by Christine Berrington
Food photography by Peter Barry
Edited by Ros Cocks, Jillian Stewart and Kate Cranshaw

CLB 3279

This 1993 edition published by Magna Books, Magna Road, Wigston, Leicester LE18 4ZH.

Printed and bound in Singapore.
ISBN 1 85422 595 2

INDIAN COOKING

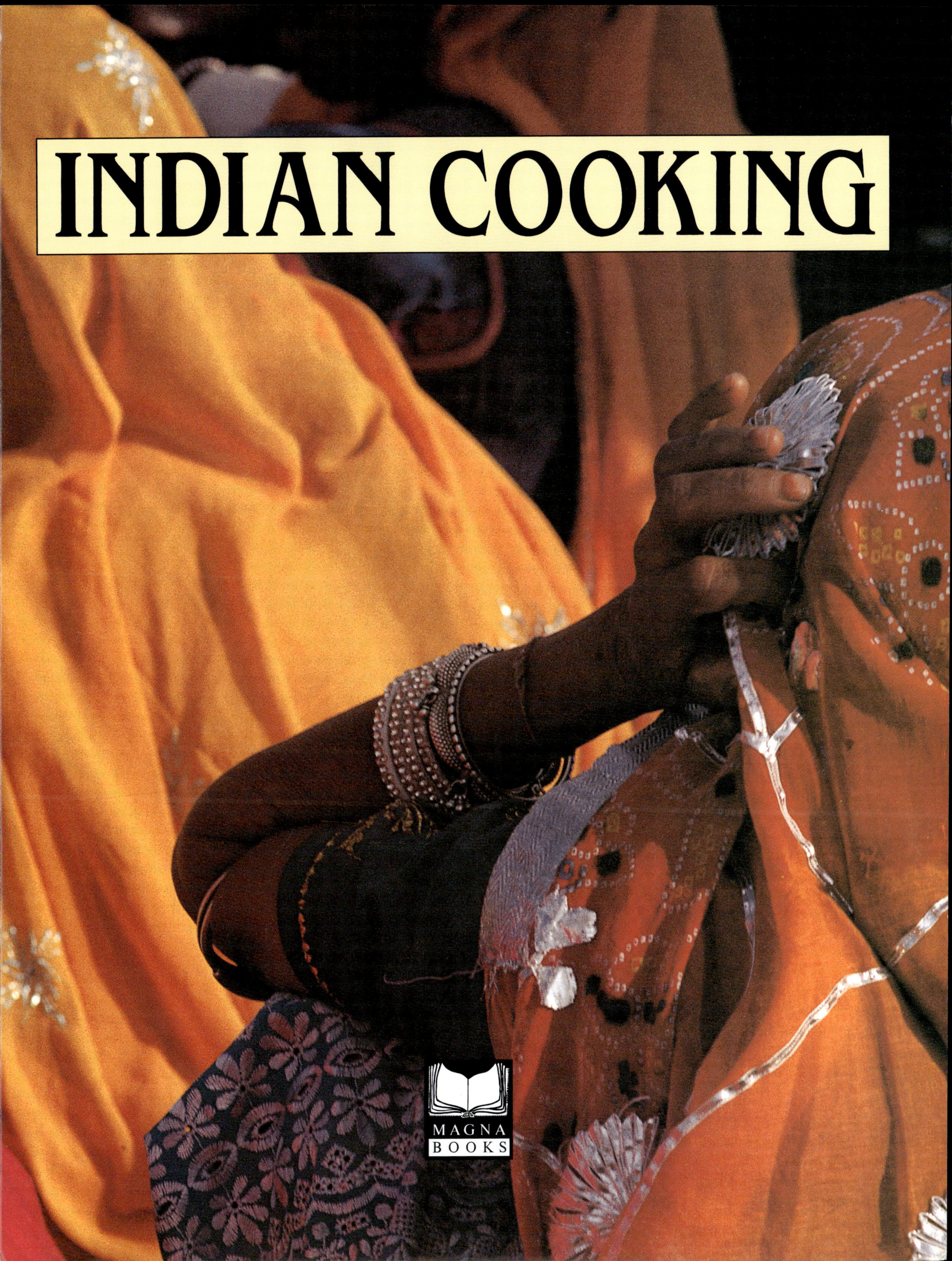

MAGNA BOOKS

INTRODUCTION

Indian cooking in Britain stems from colonial days. In the West, the eating of Indian food was once only the domain of the ex-empire builders whose memsahibs brought back recipes for curries from India to Britain. However, the spices were not available here in those early days, and the resulting British curries were insipid and generally not too inspiring. In the 1950s, Indian and Pakistani workers came to Britain, and as a result Indian restaurants sprang up, inevitably gaining popularity amongst a population who had been languishing on a bland post-war diet.

Today, there are Indian restaurants in every town, some very fashionable and expensive, others still cheap and cheerful. As proprietary curry powders began to appear in the shops, so people began to experiment at making their own curries and rice dishes. This fascination has developed and matured over the years and at last it is relatively easy to find the separate spices and other ingredients necessary for authentic Indian cookery.

Many supermarkets stock most spices needed for the curries in this book such as chilli powder, cumin, coriander, turmeric, cinnamon and cloves, as well as fresh produce such as coriander leaves, root ginger and green chillies. You may have to hunt further for some, such as fenugreek, cardamom, and special flours such as atta flour for chappatties and gram flour for bhajiyas. For these things you may have to seek out an Indian grocer, which is easier in some areas than others, depending on the local population.

Spices do not keep their aroma for long once ground, so ground spices should be bought regularly and in small quantities. The best flavours are obtained by buying whole spices and grinding them yourself at home, as and when you need them. For these recipes it is recommended that you have an electric coffee grinder for spice grinding, and a liquidizer is often required for blending together ingredients such as garlic, ginger and coriander leaves.

Indian cooking is not as complicated as some people imagine, and the preparation of the spices – the crushing, grinding and roasting – is immensely satisfying and of far greater therapeutic value than simply reaching for the tin of curry powder. Other sceptics feel they would never adapt to the spiciness and heat involved in eating chillies. They may well be right, but many Indian dishes, especially those from the north of India, such as the Korma, are only lightly spiced – not necessarily 'hot' at all – and come in thick creamy sauces. It is in southern India, where life is hotter and harsher, that they like highly spiced drier curries, such as the Madras.

This book contains a whole spectrum of delicious Indian dishes. There are irresistible little spicy starters, such as Onion Bhajiyas; a wide selection of main dishes based on fish, vegetables, poultry and meat; as well rice and Indian breads such as Chappatties or Naan. There are also some lovely side-dishes and desserts, including the wonderful Kulfi – a delectable Indian version of ice cream. The recipes are concise and easy to follow, and will inspire and embolden even the most timid cooks to broaden their culinary repertoire.

Masala Machchi

Preparation Time: 15-20 minutes, plus 2-3 hours marinating time
Cooking Time: 12-15 minutes **Serves:** 4

Masala Machchi or spicy fish is made by marinating fish in lemon juice and spices. The lemon juice gives the fish a rather smooth and velvety texture.

Ingredients

Juice of ½ lemon
1 small onion, coarsely chopped
2-3 cloves garlic, coarsely chopped
2.5cm/1-inch cube of root ginger, coarsely chopped
1-2 fresh green chillies, chopped, and seeded if a milder flavour is preferred
3 tbsps chopped coriander leaves
1 tsp salt or to taste
450g/1lb fillet of any white fish
90ml/6 tbsps oil for shallow frying

To coat the fish

3 tbsps plain flour
¼ tsp salt
¼ tsp chilli powder
1 egg, beaten

Put the lemon juice, onion, garlic, ginger, green chillies, coriander leaves and 1 tsp salt into a liquidiser and blend until smooth. Wash the fish gently and pat dry with absorbent paper. If you are using frozen fish, defrost thoroughly and then dry as for fresh fish. Cut the fish into 3.75×2.5cm/1½×1-inch pieces. Put a light coating of the spice paste on all sides of each piece of fish, cover the container and leave to marinate in a cool place for 2-3 hours, or overnight in the refrigerator.

Mix the flour with the salt and chilli powder. Dust each piece of fish lightly with this, then dip in the beaten egg. Shallow fry in a single layer over medium heat until brown on both sides (2-3 minutes on each side). Drain on absorbent paper. Alternatively, deep fry the fish until golden brown and drain on absorbent paper.

Seekh Kababs

Preparation Time: 15-20 minutes **Cooking Time:** 35-40 minutes
Makes: 18 Kababs

Wooden skewers about 6-8 inches long are the best type of skewers for these kababs. You can use metal or steel skewers, but allow the skewers to cool before shaping the next batch of kababs onto them.

Ingredients

2 tbsps white poppy seeds
2 tbsps sesame seeds
Juice of ½ lemon
2 tbsps chopped fresh mint or 1 tsp dried or bottled mint
3-4 tbsps chopped coriander leaves
30g/1oz raw cashews
1 medium-sized onion, coarsely chopped
2 small cloves of garlic, coarsely chopped
1-2 fresh green chillies, finely chopped, and seeded if a milder flavour is preferred
675g/1½lbs lean mince, beef or lamb
2 tsps ground coriander
2 tsps ground cumin
1 tsp ground ajwain (ajowan or carum) or ground caraway seeds
½ tsp garam masala
½ tsp Tandoori colour or a few drops of red food colouring mixed with 1 tbsp tomato purée
½ tsp freshly ground black pepper
1 egg yolk
¼ tsp chilli powder
1 tsp salt or to taste
4 tbsps cooking oil

Grind the poppy and sesame seeds in a coffee grinder. Put the lemon juice, mint, coriander leaves, cashews, onion, garlic and green chillies in a food processor and liquidize to a smooth paste. Transfer the mixture to a large bowl. Using the liquidizer, grind the mince in 2-3 small batches until it is fairly smooth, rather like a paste. Add the meat to the rest of the liquidized ingredients in the bowl.

Add the rest of the ingredients, except the oil and knead the mixture until all the ingredients are mixed thoroughly and it is smooth. Alternatively, put all the ingredients, except the oil, in the food processor and liquidize until the mixture is smooth. Chill the mixture for 30 minutes.

Preheat oven to 240°C/475°F, Gas Mark 9. Line a roasting tin with aluminium foil. Divide the kabab mix into about 18 balls, each slightly larger than a golf ball. Mould a ball onto a skewer and form into a sausage shape by gently rolling between your palms (about 4-5-inches long) and place in the prepared roasting tin. Make the rest of the kababs the same way. Brush generously with the oil and place the roasting tin just below the top rung of the oven. Cook for 6-8 minutes. Remove the tin from the oven and brush the kababs liberally with the remaining oil and cook for a further 6-8 minutes. Allow the kababs to cool slightly before removing them from the skewers.

Onion Bhajiyas

Preparation Time: 15-20 minutes **Cooking Time:** 45-50 minutes **Serves:** 6-8

Onion Bhajiyas are popular all over India and have established themselves as a firm favourite in this country. They are made by coating finely shredded onions with a spicy batter.

Ingredients

180g/6oz besan (gram or chick-pea flour)
1 tsp salt or to taste
Pinch bicarbonate of soda
1 tbsp ground rice
2 tsps ground cumin
2 tsps ground coriander
½-1 tsp chilli powder
1-2 fresh green chillies, finely chopped, and seeded if a milder flavour is preferred
2 large onions, sliced into half rings and separated
200ml/⅓ pint water
Oil for deep frying

Sieve the besan and add the salt, bicarbonate of soda, ground rice, cumin, coriander, chilli powder and green chillies; mix well. Add the onions and mix again. Gradually add the water and keep mixing until a soft but thick batter is formed and the onions are thoroughly coated with this batter.

Heat the oil over medium heat (*it is important to heat the oil to the correct temperature – 160-180° C/325-350° F*). To test this, take a tiny amount of the batter, about the size of a lemon pip and drop it in the oil. If it floats up to the surface immediately but without turning brown, the oil is at the correct temperature.

Using a tablespoon put in as many small amounts (about half a tablespoonful) of the onion/batter mix as the pan will hold in a single layer. Take care not to make these amounts too large as this will result in the outside of the bhajiyas being overdone while the insides remain uncooked. Reduce the heat to low as the bhajiyas need to be fried over a gentle heat to ensure that the batter at the centre of the bhajiya is cooked, and stays soft, whilst the outside turns golden brown and crisp. This should take about 10-12 minutes for each batch. Drain the bhajiyas on absorbent paper and serve on their own with drinks or with a selection of chutneys as a starter.

Chicken Tikka

Preparation Time: 30-35 minutes, plus 6-8 hours marinating time
Cooking Time: 15-20 minutes **Serves:** 4

Chicken Tikka is one of the most popular chicken dishes cooked in the Tandoor, the Indian clay oven. This recipe is adapted to cook the chicken in the conventional oven at a high temperature.

Ingredients

450g/1lb boneless, skinned chicken breast
1 tsp salt
Juice of ½ lemon
½ tsp tandoori colour or a few drops of red food colouring mixed with 1 tbsp tomato purée
2 cloves garlic, coarsely chopped
1.25cm/½-inch cube of root ginger, coarsely chopped
2 tsps ground coriander
½ tsp ground allspice or garam masala
¼ of a whole nutmeg, finely grated
½ tsp ground turmeric
150g/5oz thick set natural yogurt
4 tbsps corn or vegetable oil
½ tsp chilli powder

Cut the chicken into 2.5cm/1-inch cubes. Sprinkle with ½ tsp salt from the specified amount, and the lemon juice – mix thoroughly, cover and keep aside for 30 minutes. Liquidize the rest of the ingredients in a food processor until smooth. Put this marinade into a sieve and hold the sieve over the chicken pieces. Press the marinade through the sieve with the back of a metal spoon until only a very coarse mixture is left.

Coat the chicken thoroughly with the sieved marinade, cover the container and leave to marinate for 6-8 hours or overnight in the refrigerator.

Preheat the oven to 230°C/450°F/Gas Mark 8. Line a roasting tin with aluminium foil (this will help to maintain the high level of temperature required to cook the chicken quickly without drying it out. Thread the chicken onto skewers, leaving a gap between each piece (this is necessary for the heat to reach all sides of the chicken). Place the skewers in the prepared roasting tin and brush with some of the remaining marinade. Cook in the centre of the oven for 6-8 minutes. Take the tin out of the oven, turn the skewers over and brush the pieces of chicken with the remaining marinade. Return the tin to the oven and cook for a further 6-8 minutes.

Shake off any excess liquid from the chicken. Place the skewers on a serving dish. You make take the tikka off the skewers if you wish, but allow the meat to cool slightly before removing from the skewers.

Chicken Chaat

Preparation Time: 15 minutes **Cooking Time:** 12-15 minutes **Serves:** 4

Recipes do not have to be elaborate to be tasty, and Chicken Chaat is a perfect example. Cubes of chicken meat, stir-fried with a light coating of spices look impressive with a colourful salad and taste superb.

Ingredients

675g/1½lbs chicken breast, skinned and boned
1 tsp salt or to taste
2-3 cloves garlic, coarsely chopped
2 tbsps cooking oil
1½ tsps ground coriander
¼ tsp ground turmeric
¼-½ tsp chilli powder
1½ tbsps lemon juice
2 tbsps finely chopped coriander leaves

Wash the chicken and dry on absorbent paper. Cut into 2.5cm/1-inch cubes. Add the salt to the garlic and crush to a smooth pulp.

Heat the oil in a frying pan, preferably non-stick or cast iron, over medium heat. Add the garlic and fry until it is lightly browned. Add the chicken and fry for 6-7 minutes, stirring constantly. Add the ground coriander, turmeric and chilli powder. Fry for 3-4 minutes, stirring frequently. Remove from heat and stir in the lemon juice and coriander leaves. Serve as a starter garnished with crispy lettuce leaves, sliced cucumber, raw sliced onion and wedges of lemon or with a selection of chutneys.

Kheema Shahzada

Preparation Time: 25-30 minutes **Cooking Time:** 40-45 minutes **Serves:** 4

Kheema, or mince, is not at all an under-rated item in Indian cookery and in fact the recipe below elevates mince to gourmet status. Do make sure that the mince is lean and that it is not too fine.

Ingredients

4 heaped tbsps ghee or unsalted butter
1 large onion, coarsely chopped
2.5cm/1-inch cube root ginger, coarsely chopped
2-4 cloves garlic, coarsely chopped

Grind the following ingredients in a coffee grinder

5cm/2-inch cinnamon stick, broken up
4 green cardamoms
4 whole cloves
4-6 dried red chillies
1 tbsp coriander seeds

Grind the following 2 ingredients separately

1 tbsp white poppy seeds
1 tbsp sesame seeds

450g/1lb lean coarse mince
½ tsp ground turmeric
1 tsp salt or to taste
60g/2oz raw cashews, split into halves
280ml/½ pint warm water
140ml/¼ pint milk
2 hard-boiled eggs, quartered lengthwise
A few sprigs of fresh coriander

Melt 2 tbsps ghee or butter over medium heat and fry the onion, ginger and garlic for about 5 minutes until the onion is soft. Squeeze out excess fat by pressing the fried ingredients onto the side of the pan with a wooden spatula and transfer them to a plate. Allow to cool.

Add the remaining ghee or butter to the pan and fry the ground ingredients, including the poppy and sesame seeds, for 1 minute, stirring constantly. Add the mince and fry about 10 minutes until all the liquid evaporates, stirring frequently. Add the turmeric, stir and fry for 30 seconds. Add the salt, cashews and the water, bring to the boil, cover the pan and cook over low heat for 15 minutes, stirring occasionally.

Meanwhile, put the milk into a liquidizer followed by the fried onions, garlic and ginger. Blend until the ingredients are smooth and stir into the mince. Bring to the boil again, cover the pan, and simmer for 10-15 minutes or until the gravy is thick. Put the mince onto a serving dish and garnish with the hard-boiled eggs and the coriander leaves.

Meat Madras

Preparation Time: 25-30 minutes **Cooking Time:** 1 hour 20 minutes
Serves: 4-6

This hot, but delicious curry is named after Madras, the major city in southern India, perhaps because in the humid south, people eat rather hot food. Strange though it may seem, this is because hot and spicy food makes one perspire, thereby cooling the body.

Ingredients

6 tbsps cooking oil
2 medium-sized onions, coarsely chopped
2.5cm/1-inch cube of root ginger, coarsely chopped
3-4 cloves garlic, coarsely chopped
4-6 dried red chillies
2 large cloves garlic, crushed
1-2 fresh green chillies, sliced lengthwise
1 × 425g/15oz can tomatoes
3 tsps ground cumin
1 tsp ground coriander
½-1 tsp chilli powder
1 tsp ground turmeric
1kg/2.2lbs leg or shoulder of lamb, fat removed and cut into 3.75cm/1½-inch cubes
175ml/6 fl oz warm water
1¼ tsps salt or to taste
1 tsp garam masala

Heat 3 tbsps oil over medium heat and fry the onions, coarsely chopped ginger, garlic and red chillies for 8-10 minutes until the onions are soft, stirring frequently. Remove from heat and allow to cool.

Meanwhile, heat the remaining oil over medium heat and fry the crushed garlic and green chillies until the garlic is lightly browned. Add half the tomatoes, along with the juice; stir and cook for 1-2 minutes. Add the cumin, coriander, chilli powder and turmeric, adjust heat to low and cook for 6-8 minutes, stirring frequently. Add the meat and adjust heat to medium-high. Stir and fry for 5-6 minutes until meat changes colour. Add the water, bring to the boil, cover and simmer for 30 minutes.

Place the fried onion mixture in a liquidizer and add the remaining tomatoes. Blend until smooth and add this to the meat. Bring to the boil, add salt and mix well. Cover the pan and simmer for a further 35-40 minutes or until the meat is tender. Stir in the garam masala, remove from the heat and serve with plain boiled rice or any Indian bread.

Egg and Potato Dum

Preparation Time: 15 minutes **Cooking Time:** 35-40 minutes **Serves:** 4-6

Hard-boiled curried eggs are very popular in the northeastern part of India. Here, the eggs are cooked with potatoes and they are both fried first until they form a light crust. Slow cooking, without any loss of steam, is the secret of the success of this dish.

Ingredients

6 hard-boiled eggs
5 tbsps cooking oil
450g/1lb medium-sized potatoes, quartered
large pinch each of chilli powder and ground turmeric, mixed together
1 large onion, finely chopped
1.25cm/½-inch cube of root ginger, grated
5cm/2-inch cinnamon stick, broken into 2-3 pieces
2 black cardamoms, split open
4 whole cloves
1 fresh green chilli, chopped
1 × 425g/15oz can tomatoes
½ tsp ground turmeric
2 tsps ground coriander
1 tsp ground fennel
¼-½ tsp chilli powder (optional)
1 tsp salt or to taste
200ml/⅓ pint warm water
1 tbsp chopped coriander leaves

Shell the eggs and make 4 slits lengthwise on each egg leaving about 1.25cm/½-inch gap on either end. Heat the oil over medium heat in a cast iron or non-stick pan (enamel or steel pans will cause the eggs and the potatoes to stick). Fry the potatoes for about 10 minutes until they are well browned on all sides. Remove them with a slotted spoon and keep aside. Remove the pan from heat and stir in the turmeric and chilli mixture. Place the pan back on heat and fry the whole eggs until they are well browned. Remove them with a slotted spoon and keep aside.

In the same oil, fry the onion, ginger, cinnamon, cardamom, cloves and green chilli for 6-7 minutes until the onion is lightly browned. Add half the tomatoes, stir and fry for 2-3 minutes until the tomatoes break up. Add the turmeric, ground coriander, fennel and chilli powder (if used); stir and fry for 3-4 minutes. Add the rest of the tomatoes and fry for 4-5 minutes, stirring frequently. Add the potatoes, salt and water, bring to the boil, cover the pan tightly and simmer until the potatoes are tender, stirring occasionally.

Add the eggs and simmer, uncovered for 5-6 minutes, stirring once or twice. Stir in the coriander leaves and remove from heat.

Meat Vindaloo

Preparation Time: 10-15 minutes, plus 4-6 hours marinating time **Cooking Time:** 1 hour 15 minutes **Serves:** 4-6

Vindaloo is made by marinating the meat in vinegar and spices. It is traditionally a hot curry, but the quantity of chillies can be adjusted to suit individual taste.

Ingredients

Grind the following 5 ingredients in a coffee grinder

2 tbsps coriander seeds
1 tbsp cumin seeds
6-8 dried red chillies
1 tbsp mustard seeds
½ tsp fenugreek seeds

3-4 tbsps cider or white wine vinegar
1 tsp ground turmeric
2.5cm/1-inch cube of root ginger, finely grated
3-4 cloves garlic, crushed
1kg/2.2lbs shoulder of lamb or beef stewing steak
4 tbsps cooking oil
1 large onion, finely chopped
1-2 tsps chilli powder
1 tsp paprika
1¼ tsps salt or to taste
430ml/¾ pint warm water
2-3 medium-sized potatoes
1 tbsp chopped coriander leaves (optional)

In a large bowl, make a thick paste out of the ground spices, by adding the vinegar. Add the turmeric, ginger and garlic. Mix thoroughly. Trim off excess fat from the meat and cut into 2.5cm/1-inch cubes. Add the meat and mix it well so that all the pieces are fully coated with the paste. Cover the bowl with cling film and leave to marinate for 4-6 hours or overnight in the refrigerator.

Put the meat in a pan and place this over medium heat, allow the meat to heat through, stirring occasionally; this will take about 5 minutes. Cover the pan, and cook the meat in its own juice for 15-20 minutes or until the liquid is reduced to a thick paste. Stir occasionally during this time to ensure that the meat does not stick to the bottom of the pan. Remove from heat and keep aside.

Heat the oil over medium heat and fry the onion for about 5 minutes until it is soft. Add the meat and fry for 6-8 minutes stirring frequently. Add the chilli powder, paprika and salt. Stir and fry for a further 2-3 minutes. Add the water, bring to the boil, cover and simmer for 40-45 minutes or until the meat is nearly tender (beef will take longer than lamb, check water level and add more water if necessary).

Meanwhile, peel and wash the potatoes. Cut them into approximately 3.75cm/1½-inch cubes. Add this to the meat and bring to the boil again. Cover the pan and simmer for 15-20 minutes until the potatoes are cooked. Turn the vindaloo on to a serving dish and sprinkle the coriander leaves on top.

Fish Bhoona

Preparation Time: 15-20 minutes **Cooking Time:** 30-35 minutes **Serves:** 4

A spicy coating and aromatic tomato sauce transform chunks of white fish in this simple recipe.

Ingredients

675g/1½lbs steak or fillets of any white fish
6 tbsps cooking oil

Mix the following 4 ingredients in a small bowl

1 tbsp plain flour
¼ tsp ground turmeric
¼ tsp chilli powder
¼ tsp salt

1 large onion, coarsely chopped
1.25cm/½-inch cube of root ginger, coarsely chopped
2-4 cloves garlic, coarsely chopped
½ tsp ground turmeric
¼ tsp chilli powder
1 tsp ground coriander
½ tsp garam masala
1 × 425g/15oz can of tomatoes
150ml/5 fl oz warm water
120g/4oz frozen garden peas
1 tsp salt or to taste
1 tbsp chopped coriander leaves

Skin the fish, wash and dry thoroughly on absorbent paper and cut the fish into approximately 2.5 × 5cm/1 × 2-inch pieces. Heat 2 tbsps oil in a large frying pan, preferably non-stick or cast iron, over medium heat. Lightly dust the fish, one piece at a time, in the seasoned flour and place in the hot oil. Put in as many pieces as the pan will hold in a single layer without overcrowding it and adjust heat to medium-high. Fry the fish until all the pieces are evenly browned. This has to be done quickly in fairly hot oil so that the fish is thoroughly sealed. Fry all the fish this way and drain on absorbent paper.

Put the onion, ginger and garlic into a liquidiser and blend until smooth. Heat the remaining oil over medium heat in a wide, shallow pan. Add the onion mixture and stir. When the mixture is heated through turn heat down to low, stir and fry for 3-4 minutes. Add the turmeric, chilli, coriander and garam masala and fry for 4-5 minutes, stirring continuously. During this time, from the tin of tomatoes, add 1 tbsp juice at a time to prevent the spices from sticking to the bottom of the pan. Then, add one tomato at a time, along with any remaining juice, breaking the tomato with the back of the spoon. Cook until the tomato is well incorporated into the rest of the ingredients. Use up the rest of the tomatoes in the same way. Add the water, peas and salt. Bring to the boil and add the fish. Cover and simmer for 5 to 6 minutes. Remove from heat and sprinkle the coriander leaves on top.

Coriander Chicken

Preparation Time: 20 minutes, plus 2-4 hours marinating time **Cooking Time:** 45-50 minutes **Serves:** 4-6

Coriander Chicken is quick and easy to make, it tastes wonderful and looks very impressive – a perfect choice for any dinner party menu.

Ingredients

1kg/2.2lbs chicken joints, skinned
2-4 cloves garlic, crushed
150ml/5 fl oz thick set natural yogurt
5 tbsps cooking oil
1 large onion, finely sliced
2 tbsps ground coriander
½ tsp ground black pepper
1 tsp ground mixed spice
½ tsp ground turmeric
½ tsp cayenne pepper or chilli powder
120ml/4 fl oz warm water
1 tsp salt or to taste
30g/1oz ground almonds
2 hard-boiled eggs, sliced
¼ tsp paprika

Cut each chicken joint into two, mix thoroughly with the crushed garlic and the yogurt. Cover the container and leave to marinate in a cool place for 2-4 hours or overnight in the refrigerator.

Heat the oil over medium heat and fry the onion for 6-8 minutes until it is golden brown. Remove with a slotted spoon and keep aside. In the same oil, fry the coriander, ground pepper, ground mixed spice and turmeric for 15 seconds and add the chicken along with all the marinade in the container. Adjust heat to medium-high and fry the chicken for 5-6 minutes until it changes colour. Add the cayenne or chilli powder, water, salt, and the fried onion slices. Bring to the boil, cover the pan and simmer until the chicken is tender (about 30 minutes).

Stir in the ground almonds, remove from heat and serve garnished with the hard-boiled eggs and sprinkled with paprika.

Pasanda Badam Curry

Preparation Time: 30 minutes **Cooking Time:** 1 hour 20 minutes **Serves:** 4-6

Pasanda is a classic north Indian dish where the meat is cut into thin slices and cooked in a rich sauce containing saffron, yogurt and cream.

Ingredients

900g/2lbs boned leg of lamb
2.5cm/1-inch cube root ginger, coarsely chopped
4-6 cloves garlic, coarsely chopped
2 fresh green chillies, seeded and coarsely chopped
4 tbsps natural yogurt
60g/2oz ghee or unsalted butter
3 medium-sized onions, finely sliced
½ tsp ground turmeric
1 tsp ground cumin
2 tsps ground coriander
½ tsp ground nutmeg
¼-½ tsp chilli powder
200ml/⅓ pint warm water
1¼ tsps salt or to taste
150ml/5 fl oz single cream
30g/1oz ground almonds
1 tsp garam masala or ground mixed spice
2 tbsps rosewater
½ tsp paprika

Beat the meat with a meat mallet to flatten it to 5mm/¼-inch thickness, then cut into thin slices (about 3.75cm/1½-inch long and 1.25cm/½-inch wide). Put the ginger, garlic, green chillies and yogurt into a liquidizer and blend until smooth.

Melt the ghee or butter over medium heat and fry the onions for 6-8 minutes until they are lightly browned. Add the turmeric, cumin, coriander, nutmeg and chilli powder; adjust heat to low, stir and fry for 2-3 minutes. Add the meat and fry it over high heat for 3-4 minutes or until it changes colour. Add about 2 tbsps of the liquidized ingredients and cook for 1-2 minutes, stirring frequently. Repeat this process until all the yogurt mixture is used up. Fry the meat over medium heat for 4-5 minutes stirring frequently. When the fat begins to seep through the thick spice paste and floats on the surface, add the water, bring to the boil, cover the pan and simmer for about 60 minutes until the meat is tender, stirring occasionally.

Add the salt, cream and ground almonds and let it simmer without the lid for 5-6 minutes. Stir in the garam masala and rosewater and remove from heat. Put the pasanda into a serving dish and sprinkle the paprika on top.

Prawn Chilli Masala

Preparation Time: 15 minutes **Cooking Time:** 20-25 minutes **Serves:** 4

This is a delicate but richly flavoured dish. Traditionally, in India, only fresh and juicy king prawns will do, but standard peeled prawns can be used for this recipe.

Ingredients

90g/3oz unsalted butter
6 green cardamoms, split open
2.5cm/1-inch cube of root ginger, finely grated
3-4 cloves garlic, crushed
1 tbsp ground coriander
½ tsp ground turmeric
450g/1lb fresh peeled prawns
150ml/5 fl oz thick set natural yogurt
90ml/3 fl oz water
1 tsp sugar
1 tsp salt or to taste
30g/1oz ground almonds
4-6 whole fresh green chillies
120g/4oz finely chopped onions
2 fresh green chillies, seeded and minced
½ tsp garam masala
1 tbsp chopped coriander leaves

Melt 60g/2oz butter over gentle heat and add the whole cardamoms, fry for 30 seconds and add the ginger and garlic. Stir and cook for 1 minute, then add the ground coriander and turmeric. Stir and fry for 30 seconds. Add the prawns, turn the heat up to medium and cook for 5-6 minutes, stirring frequently.

Beat the yogurt until smooth, gradually add the water and beat until well blended. Add this mixture to the prawns, stir in the sugar and the salt, cover the pan and simmer for 5-6 minutes. Add the ground almonds and the whole green chillies and cook, uncovered, for 5 minutes.

Meanwhile, fry the onion in the remaining butter until just soft, but not brown. Add the minced green chillies and the garam masala; stir and fry for a further 1-2 minutes. Stir this mixture into the prawns along with any butter left in the pan. Remove the pan from the heat. Put the prawns in a serving dish and garnish with the coriander leaves.

Kofta Bhoona

Preparation Time: 25-30 minutes **Cooking Time:** 50-55 minutes **Serves:** 4-6

Kofta Bhoona consists of tiny meatballs the size of marbles which are coated with a delicious spice paste.

Ingredients

450g/1lb fine lean mince, lamb or beef
1 large clove garlic, crushed
1 tsp garam masala
1-2 fresh green chillies, seeded and minced
1½ tsps salt or to taste
2 tbsps fresh coriander leaves, minced
3 tbsps cooking oil
1 large onion, finely chopped
5mm/¼-inch cube root ginger, grated
2 tsps ground coriander
1 tsp ground cumin

Make a paste of the following 5 ingredients

½-1 tsp chilli powder
2 cloves garlic, crushed
½ tsp ground turmeric
2 tbsps tomato purée
120ml/4 fl oz cold water

200ml/⅓ pint warm water
60g/2oz frozen garden peas
¼ tsp garam masala
2 tbsps chopped coriander leaves

Put the mince in a large bowl and add the garlic, garam masala, green chillies, 1 tsp salt and the coriander leaves. Mix the ingredients thoroughly and knead the mince until it is smooth. Divide the mixture into about 28-30 marble-sized balls (koftas). Make the koftas by rolling the balls between the palms in a circular motion until they are smooth and round.

Heat the oil over medium heat, preferably in a nonstick or cast iron pan, and fry the koftas in 2-3 batches. Turn the koftas as they brown and when they are brown all over, remove with a slotted spoon and drain on absorbent paper. In the same oil, fry the onion and ginger for 6-8 minutes stirring frequently until the onion is golden brown. Adjust heat to low and add the ground coriander, stir and fry for 30 seconds. Add the ground cumin and fry for 30 seconds. Adjust heat to medium and add 2 tbsps of the tomato purée mixture. Stir and fry until it dries up. Repeat the process until all the tomato purée mixture is used up. Add the warm water and the remaining salt and bring to the boil. Add the koftas, cover the pan and simmer for 10 minutes.

Adjust heat to medium, bring the liquid to the boil, stir and cook for 4-5 minutes. Add the peas and the garam masala and continue to cook, uncovered, until the gravy is fairly thick, stirring frequently. Stir in the coriander leaves, remove from heat and serve.

Mixed Vegetable Curry

Preparation Time: 25-30 minutes **Cooking Time:** 30 minutes **Serves:** 4-6

A variety of seasonal vegetables are cooked together in a gravy flavoured by a few ground spices, onions and tomatoes. Whole green chillies are added towards the end to enhance the flavour of the dish and also to retain their fresh green colour.

Ingredients

4-5 tbsps cooking oil
1 large onion, finely chopped
1.25cm/½-inch cube of root ginger, finely sliced
1 tsp ground turmeric
1 tsp ground coriander
1 tsp ground cumin
1 tsp paprika
4 small ripe tomatoes, skinned and chopped, or 1 × 425g/15oz can of tomatoes
225g/8oz potatoes, diced
90g/3oz french beans or dwarf beans, sliced
120g/4oz carrots, sliced
90g/3oz shelled garden peas
430ml/¾ pint warm water
2-4 whole fresh green chillies
1 tsp garam masala
1 tsp salt or to taste
1 tbsp chopped coriander leaves

Heat the oil over medium heat and fry the onion for 6-7 minutes until lightly browned. Add the ginger and fry for 30 seconds. Adjust heat to low and add the turmeric, coriander, cumin and paprika. Stir and mix well. Add half the tomatoes and fry for 2 minutes, stirring continuously. Add all the vegetables and the water. Stir and mix well. Bring to the boil, cover and simmer for 15-20 minutes until vegetables are tender.

Add the remaining tomatoes and the green chillies. Cover and simmer for 5-6 minutes. Add the garam masala and salt, mix well. Stir in half the coriander leaves and remove from heat. Put the vegetable curry into a serving dish and sprinkle the remaining coriander leaves on top.

Rogan Josh

Preparation Time: 20 minutes **Cooking Time:** 1 hour 30 minutes **Serves:** 4-6

Rogan Josh finds its origin in Kashmir, the northern-most state in India. In the recipe below, more than the usual quantity of spices are used, but these are toned down by using a large quantity of tomatoes and a little double cream.

Ingredients

3 tbsps ghee or unsalted butter
1 kg/2.2lbs leg of lamb, without bones, cut into 3.75cm/1½-inch cubes
1 tbsp ground cumin
1 tbsp ground coriander
1 tsp ground turmeric
1 tsp chilli powder
2.5cm/1-inch cube of root ginger, grated
2-4 cloves garlic, crushed
225g-275g/8-10oz onion, finely sliced
1 × 425g/15oz can of tomatoes, chopped or whole
1 tbsp tomato purée
120ml/4 fl oz warm water
1¼ tsps salt or to taste
90ml/3 fl oz double cream
2 tsps garam masala
2 tbsps chopped coriander leaves

Melt 2 tbsps ghee or butter over medium heat and fry the meat in 2-3 batches until it changes colour. Remove each batch with a slotted spoon and keep aside. Lower heat to minimum and add the cumin, coriander, turmeric, chilli powder, ginger and garlic. Stir and fry for 30 seconds. Adjust heat to medium and add the meat along with all the ghee and juice in the container. Stir and fry for 3-4 minutes and add the onion. Fry for 5-6 minutes stirring frequently. Add the tomatoes and tomato purée, stir and cook for 2-3 minutes. Add the water and salt, bring to the boil, cover and simmer for about 60 minutes until the meat is tender. Stir in the cream and remove from heat.

In a separate pan melt the remaining ghee over medium heat and add the garam masala, stir briskly and add to the meat. Transfer a little meat gravy to the pan in which the garam masala was fried, stir thoroughly to ensure that any remaining garam masala and ghee mixture is fully incorporated into the gravy, and add this to the meat. Mix well.Stir in the coriander leaves and serve with plain boiled rice.

Meat Dilpasand

Preparation Time: 20 minutes, plus 4-6 hours marinating time **Cooking Time:** 1 hour 45 minutes **Serves:** 4-6

A delectable lamb dish with a slightly creamy texture and a wonderfully nutty flavour derived from roasted and ground poppy seeds.

Ingredients

1kg/2.2lbs leg of lamb
150ml/5 fl oz thick set natural yogurt
1 tsp ground turmeric
2 tbsps white poppy seeds
2.5cm/1-inch cube root ginger, coarsely chopped
4-5 cloves garlic, coarsely chopped
1-2 fresh green chillies, seeded if a milder flavour is preferred
450g/1lb onions
3 tbsps ghee or unsalted butter
½ tsp chilli powder
1 tsp paprika
1 tbsp ground cumin
1 tsp garam masala
1 tbsp tomato purée
1¼ tsps salt or to taste
175ml/6 fl oz warm water
30g/1oz creamed coconut or 2 tbsps desiccated coconut
2 tbsps chopped coriander leaves

Trim off any fat from the meat, wash and dry on absorbent paper and cut into 3.75cm/1½-inch cubes. Add yogurt and turmeric, mix thoroughly, cover the container and leave to marinate for 4-6 hours or overnight in the refrigerator.

Roast the poppy seeds without fat over gentle heat until they are a shade darker, and allow to cool. Place the ginger, garlic and green chillies in a liquidizer. Chop 1 onion and add to the ginger and garlic mixture. Blend until fairly smooth. Chop the remaining onions finely. Melt the ghee or butter over medium heat and fry these onions until golden brown. This will take 10 to 12 minutes. Adjust heat to low and add chilli powder, paprika, cumin and ½ tsp garam masala. Stir and fry for 2-3 minutes. Add the liquidized ingredients and fry for 10 to 12 minutes, stirring frequently. If during this time the spices tend to stick to the bottom of the pan, sprinkle with about 1 tbsp of water at a time as and when necessary. Add the meat and adjust heat to medium-high. Fry for 4-5 minutes stirring constantly. Add the tomato purée, salt and water, stir and mix, bring to the boil, cover and simmer for 45 minutes or until the meat is tender. Stir occasionally during the first half of cooking, but more frequently towards the end to ensure that the thickened gravy does not stick to the bottom of the pan.

If you are using creamed coconut, cut into small pieces with a sharp knife. Desiccated coconut should be ground in the coffee grinder before use to ensure that the necessary fine texture is achieved in making the curry. Finish off the cooking process in the same way as for creamed coconut. Grind the poppy seeds in a coffee grinder and stir into the meat along with the creamed coconut. Stir until coconut is dissolved. Cover and simmer for 15 minutes. Stir in the coriander leaves and the remaining garam masala. Remove from heat and serve.

Chicken with Whole Spices

Preparation Time: 15-20 minutes **Cooking Time:** 50 minutes **Serves:** 4-6

This recipe is the answer to a good, tasty curry in a hurry! With this curry on the menu, you can present a whole meal in approximately one hour.

Ingredients

1kg/2.2lbs chicken joints, skinned
4 tbsps cooking oil
1 tsp cumin seeds
1 large onion, finely chopped
1.25cm/½-inch cube of root ginger, finely chopped
2-4 cloves garlic, crushed or finely chopped
2-3 dried red chillies, whole
2 × 5cm/2-inch cinnamon sticks, broken
2 black cardamoms, split open
4 whole cloves
10 whole allspice seeds
½ tsp ground turmeric
1 tsp paprika
140ml/¼ pint warm water
1¼ tsps salt or to taste
2 ripe tomatoes, skinned and chopped
2 fresh green chillies, whole
1 tbsp ground almonds
2 tbsps chopped coriander leaves (optional)

Cut each chicken joint in two; separate leg from thigh and cut each breast in two. Heat the oil over medium heat and fry the cumin seeds until they pop, then add the onion, ginger, garlic and red chillies. Fry until the onion is soft but not brown, stirring frequently. Add the cinnamon, cardamom, cloves and allspice, stir and fry for 30 seconds. Stir in the turmeric and paprika and immediately follow with the chicken. Adjust heat to medium-high and fry the chicken for 5-6 minutes until it changes colour, stirring frequently. Add the water and salt, bring to the boil, cover the pan and simmer for about 30 minutes until the chicken is tender.

Add the tomatoes, green chillies and the ground almonds. Stir and mix well, cover the pan and simmer for a further 6-8 minutes. Stir in half the coriander leaves and remove the pan from heat. Transfer the chicken into a serving dish and garnish with the remaining coriander leaves, if required.

Rogan Josh

Preparation Time: 20 minutes **Cooking Time:** 1 hour 30 minutes **Serves:** 4-6

Rogan Josh finds its origin in Kashmir, the northern-most state in India. In the recipe below, more than the usual quantity of spices are used, but these are toned down by using a large quantity of tomatoes and a little double cream.

Ingredients

3 tbsps ghee or unsalted butter
1 kg/2.2lbs leg of lamb, without bones, cut into 3.75cm/1½-inch cubes
1 tbsp ground cumin
1 tbsp ground coriander
1 tsp ground turmeric
1 tsp chilli powder
2.5cm/1-inch cube of root ginger, grated
2-4 cloves garlic, crushed
225g-275g/8-10oz onion, finely sliced
1 × 425g/15oz can of tomatoes, chopped or whole
1 tbsp tomato purée
120ml/4 fl oz warm water
1¼ tsps salt or to taste
90ml/3 fl oz double cream
2 tsps garam masala
2 tbsps chopped coriander leaves

Melt 2 tbsps ghee or butter over medium heat and fry the meat in 2-3 batches until it changes colour. Remove each batch with a slotted spoon and keep aside. Lower heat to minimum and add the cumin, coriander, turmeric, chilli powder, ginger and garlic. Stir and fry for 30 seconds. Adjust heat to medium and add the meat along with all the ghee and juice in the container. Stir and fry for 3-4 minutes and add the onion. Fry for 5-6 minutes stirring frequently. Add the tomatoes and tomato purée, stir and cook for 2-3 minutes. Add the water and salt, bring to the boil, cover and simmer for about 60 minutes until the meat is tender. Stir in the cream and remove from heat.

In a separate pan melt the remaining ghee over medium heat and add the garam masala, stir briskly and add to the meat. Transfer a little meat gravy to the pan in which the garam masala was fried, stir thoroughly to ensure that any remaining garam masala and ghee mixture is fully incorporated into the gravy, and add this to the meat. Mix well.Stir in the coriander leaves and serve with plain boiled rice.

Shahi Korma

Preparation Time: 20-25 minutes, plus 2-4 hours marinating time
Cooking Time: 1½ hours **Serves:** 4-6

The word 'Shahi' means royal, so the title itself is evidence that this particular korma was created in the royal kitchens of the great Maharajas of India. The dish is rich and creamy and is a perfect choice for a special occasion.

Ingredients

1kg/2.2lbs boned leg of lamb, fat trimmed and cut into 3.75cm/1½-inch cubes
150ml/5 fl oz thick set natural yogurt
1.25cm/½-inch cube of root ginger, grated
3-4 cloves garlic, crushed
60g/2oz ghee or unsalted butter
2 medium-sized onions, finely chopped

Grind the following ingredients in a coffee grinder

2 tbsps coriander seeds
8 green cardamoms
10 whole black peppercorns
3-4 dried red chillies

Mix the following 2 spices with the above ground ingredients

1 tsp ground cinnamon
1 tsp ground mace

3-4 tbsps chopped fresh mint or 1½ tsps dried or bottled mint
60g/2oz ground almonds
280ml/½ pint warm water
½ tsp saffron strands, crushed
1½ tsps salt or to taste
60g/2oz raw split cashews
150ml/5 fl oz single cream
1 tbsp rosewater

Put the meat into a bowl and add the yogurt, ginger and garlic. Mix thoroughly, cover the bowl with cling film and leave to marinate for 2-4 hours or overnight in the refrigerator.

Put the marinated meat, along with any remaining marinade in the container, in a heavy-based saucepan and place it over medium-low heat. Bring to a slow simmer, cover, and cook the meat in its own juice for 45-50 minutes stirring occasionally. Remove the pan from the heat and lift the meat with a slotted spoon. Transfer the meat to another container and keep hot.

Melt the ghee over medium heat and fry the onions for 8-9 minutes until they are lightly browned. Adjust heat to low and add the ground ingredients and the mint; stir and fry for 2-3 minutes. Add the half of the liquid in which the meat was cooked, stir and cook for 1-2 minutes. Add the ground almonds and mix thoroughly; add the remaining meat stock, stir and cook for a further 1-2 minutes. Adjust heat to medium and add the meat, stir and fry the meat for 5-6 minutes. Add the water, saffron strands, salt and cashews, bring the liquid to a slow boil, cover and simmer for 20 minutes.

Add the cream, stir and mix well, simmer uncovered for 6-8 minutes. Stir in the rosewater and remove from the heat and serve.

Meat Samosas

Preparation Time: 30 minutes **Cooking Time:** 40 minutes
Makes: 18 Samosas

These ever popular samosas make a wonderful treat on any occasion and are particularly appreciated at buffets and cocktail parties.

Ingredients

2 tbsps cooking oil
2 medium-sized onions, finely chopped
225g/8oz lean mince, lamb or beef
3-4 cloves garlic, crushed
½-inch cube of root ginger, finely grated
½ tsp ground turmeric
2 tsps ground coriander
1½ tsps ground cumin
½-1 tsp chilli powder
½ tsp salt or to taste
120ml/4 fl oz warm water
150g/5oz frozen garden peas
2 tbsps desiccated coconut
1 tsp garam masala
1-2 fresh green chillies, finely chopped and seeded if a milder flavour is preferred
2 tbsps chopped coriander leaves
1 tbsp lemon juice

Pastry

225g/8oz plain flour
60g/2oz ghee or butter
½ tsp salt
75ml/2½ fl oz warm water
Oil for deep frying

Heat the oil over medium heat and fry the onions until they are lightly browned. Add the mince, garlic and ginger. Stir and fry until all the liquid evaporates and adjust heat to low. Add the turmeric, coriander, cumin, chilli powder and salt. Stir and fry until mince is lightly browned. Add the water and the peas, bring to the boil, cover and simmer for 25-30 minutes. If there is any liquid left, take the lid off and cook the mince over medium heat until it is completely dry, stirring frequently.

Stir in the coconut, garam masala, green chillies and coriander leaves. Remove from heat and add the lemon juice. Cool thoroughly before filling the Samosas.

To make the pastry, add the butter and salt to the flour. Rub in well. Mix to a soft dough by adding the water. Knead until the dough feels soft and velvety to the touch. Divide the dough into 9 balls. Rotate each ball between your palms in a circular motion, then press it down to make a flat cake. Roll out each flat cake into 4-inch discs and cut into two. Use each semicircle of pastry as one envelope. Moisten the straight edge with a little warm water. Fold the semicircle of pastry in half to form a triangular cone. Join the straight edges by pressing them hard into each other. Make sure that there are no gaps. Fill these cones with the filling, leaving about ¼-inch border on the top of the cone. Now moisten the top edges and press them hard together.

Deep fry the samosas over gentle heat until they are golden brown and drain on absorbent paper.

Pilau Rice

Preparation Time: 10 minutes, plus ½ hour soaking time **Cooking Time:** 25-30 minutes **Serves:** 4-6

Pilau is usually a beautifully fragrant rice or a combination of rice and meat, poultry, fish or vegetables. It is always cooked in pure butterfat ghee, but unsalted butter is a good substitute.

Ingredients

275g/10oz basmati rice
60g/2oz ghee or unsalted butter
1 large onion, finely sliced
2-4 cloves garlic, finely chopped
8 whole cloves
8 green cardamoms, split open
2 x 5cm/2-inch cinnamon sticks, broken up
8 whole peppercorns
1 tsp ground turmeric
570ml/1 pint water
1¼ tsps salt or to taste
1 heaped tsp butter
30g/1 oz seedless sultanas
30g/1 oz flaked almonds

Wash the rice and soak in cold water for ½ an hour. Drain well.

In a heavy-based pan melt the ghee or butter over medium heat and fry onion for about 5 minutes until it is soft but not brown. Add the garlic, cloves, cardamoms, cinnamon sticks and peppercorns. Stir and fry for 3-4 minutes until the onions are golden brown. Add the rice and turmeric, stir and fry for 1-2 minutes. Adjust heat to low, stir and fry the rice for a further 2-3 minutes. Add the water and the salt, bring to the boil, cover and simmer for 15 minutes without lifting the lid.

Remove the pan from heat and keep it undisturbed for a further 10-12 minutes. Melt the 1 tsp butter over gentle heat and fry sultanas for a minute until they change colour and swell up. Transfer the sultanas onto a plate and in the same fat fry the almonds until they are lightly browned. Remove these also to the plate. Put the pilau rice into a serving dish and, using a fork, gently mix in the fried sultanas and almonds. Serve with any meat, chicken or vegetable curry.

Saag Bhaji

Preparation Time: 25-30 minutes **Cooking Time:** 50 minutes **Serves:** 4-6

Saag Bhaji is spinach simmered in spices and combined with diced, fried potatoes.

Ingredients

6 tbsps cooking oil
½ tsp black mustard seeds
1 tsp cumin seeds
8-10 fenugreek seeds (optional)
1 tbsp curry leaves
2-3 cloves garlic, finely chopped
2-4 dried red chillies, coarsely chopped
450g/1lb fresh leaf spinach or 225g/8oz frozen leaf spinach, finely chopped
1 tbsp ghee or unsalted butter
1 large potato, diced
1 large onion, finely sliced
½ tsp ground turmeric
1 tsp ground cumin
½ tsp garam masala
¼-½ tsp chilli powder
2-3 ripe tomatoes, skinned and chopped
1 tsp salt or to taste

Heat 2 tbsps oil over medium heat and fry mustard seeds until they pop. Add the cumin seeds, fenugreek (if used) and curry leaves and immediately follow with the garlic and red chillies. Allow garlic to turn slightly brown. Add the spinach, stir and mix thoroughly. Cover and simmer for 15 minutes, stirring occasionally.

Melt the ghee or butter over medium heat and brown the diced potatoes. Remove from heat and keep aside. Heat the remaining oil over medium heat and fry onion for about 10 minutes until well browned, take care not to burn the onion or it will taste bitter. Adjust heat to minimum and add turmeric, cumin, garam masala and chilli powder, stir and fry for 2-3 minutes. Add the spinach, potatoes, tomatoes and salt, cover and simmer for 10 minutes or until the potatoes are tender, stirring occasionally. Remove from heat and serve.

Chapatties

Preparation Time: 20-25 minutes, plus ½-1 hour resting time **Cooking Time:** 35-40 minutes **Makes:** 14 Chapatties

A Chapattie is a dry roasted unleavened bread best eaten as soon as it is cooked. Allow 2-3 chapatties per person.

Ingredients

340g/12oz fine wholemeal flour or Atta/Chapatti flour
½ tsp salt
1 tbsp butter or ghee
200-280ml/⅓-½ pint warm water (quantity depends on the texture of the flour)
1 tbsp extra flour in a shallow bowl or plate.

Food Mixer Method

Place the flour, salt and fat together in the bowl and mix thoroughly at the medium-to-low speed taking care to see that all the fat has been broken up and well incorporated into the flour. Turn speed down to minimum and gradually add the water. When the dough is formed, knead it until it is soft and pliable. Cover the dough with a well-moistened cloth and keep aside for ½-1 hour.

Hand Method

Put the flour and salt in a large bowl and rub in the fat. Gradually add the water and keep mixing and kneading until a soft and pliable dough is formed. Cover the dough as above and keep aside.

Divide the dough into 14 walnut-sized portions. Roll each portion in a circular motion between the palms to make a smooth round ball, then flatten the ball to make a round cake. Dip each cake into the dry flour and roll the chapatti disc of about 15cm/6-inch diameter.

An iron griddle is normally used for cooking chapattis, but if you do not have one, then make sure you use a heavy-based frying pan as the chapatties need even distribution of heat during cooking. Overheating of the pan will cause the chapatties to stick to the pan and burn. Heat the griddle or frying pan over medium heat and place a chapatti on it, cook for 30 seconds and then turn the chapatti over. Cook until brown spots appear on both sides, turning it over frequently.

To keep the chapatties warm, line a piece of aluminium foil with absorbent paper and place the chapatties on one end, cover with the other and seal the edges. Serve with any meat, chicken or vegetable curry.

Cucumber and Onion Raita

Preparation Time: 10-15 minutes **Serves:** 4-6

Raitas and salads are an integral part of an Indian meal. This raita is particularly easy to make and the roasted cumin seeds add a special flavour.

Ingredients

1 tsp cumin seeds
150ml/5 fl oz natural yogurt
3 tbsps finely chopped onion
½ cucumber, peeled and finely chopped
½ tsp salt or to taste

Heat a cast-iron or other heavy-based pan and dry-roast the cumin seeds until they release their aroma. Allow to cool and crush them lightly.

Beat the yogurt with a fork until smooth, add the rest of the ingredients and half the crushed cumin seeds. Mix thoroughly and put in a serving dish. Sprinkle the remaining cumin seeds on top and serve with any curry, especially suitable to serve with Meat Vindaloo and Meat Madras.

Mushroom Bhaji

Preparation Time: 15 minutes **Cooking Time:** 20 minutes **Serves:** 4

Although mushrooms are not widely used in India, the Indian restaurants in this country have popularised the use of mushrooms in Indian cookery. Mushroom Bhaji appears to be one of the most popular of them all.

Ingredients

3-4 tbsps cooking oil
1 medium-sized onion, finely chopped
2-3 cloves garlic, crushed
½ tsp ground turmeric
½ tsp chilli powder
1 tsp ground coriander
1 tsp ground cumin
¾ tsp salt or to taste
1 tbsp tomato purée
225g/8oz mushrooms, chopped

Heat the oil over medium heat and fry the onion until it is lightly browned. Lower heat and add the garlic, turmeric, chilli powder, coriander and cumin. Stir and fry the spices and add about 1 tbsp water to prevent the spices from sticking to the bottom of the pan. As soon as this water dries up, add a little more. Continue doing this until you have fried the spices for about 5 minutes.

Add the salt and tomato purée, mix well and add the mushrooms. Stir until the ingredients are thoroughly mixed. Sprinkle about 2 tbsps water and cover the pan. Simmer for 10 minutes. The finished dish should have a little gravy, but it should not be runny. If it appears to be too runny, take the lid off and let the liquid evaporate until the gravy is reasonably thick. Serve with plain boiled rice or any Indian bread.

Potatoes with Garlic and Chillies

Preparation Time: 15-20 minutes **Cooking Time:** 15 minutes **Serves:** 4-6

These are rather like spicy French fries, but they are not deep fried. A perfect alternative to chips or French fries when you want a touch of spice with plain meat, fish or chicken.

Ingredients

450g/1lb potatoes
3 tbsps cooking oil
½ tsp black mustard seeds
½ tsp cumin seeds
4 cloves garlic, crushed
¼-½ tsp chilli powder
½ tsp ground turmeric
1 tsp salt or to taste

Cut the potatoes to the thickness of French fries, but half their length. In a wide, shallow non-stick or cast iron pan, heat the oil over medium heat. Add the mustard seeds and then the cumin. When the seeds start popping, add the garlic and allow it to turn lightly brown.

Remove the pan from the heat and add the chilli powder and turmeric. Add the potatoes and place the pan back on heat. Stir and turn heat up to medium. Add the salt, stir and mix, cover the pan and cook for 3-4 minutes and stir again. Continue to do this until the potatoes are cooked and lightly browned. Remove from the heat. Serve with any curry and rice or Chapatties.

Naan

Preparation Time: 10-15 minutes, plus ½-1 hour resting time **Cooking Time:** 20-25 minutes **Makes:** 8 Naan

Naan is traditionally cooked in the Tandoor. It is not difficult to cook naan in a very hot oven, although the distinctive taste of clay cooking will be missing.

Ingredients

450g/1lb plain flour
1 tsp salt
1 tsp Kalonji-onion seeds (optional)
1 tsp sugar
1½ sachets fast action or easy dissolve yeast
90ml/3 fl oz milk
150ml/5 fl oz natural yogurt
60g/2oz ghee or butter
2 tbsps sesame seeds or white poppy seeds
1 medium-sized egg, beaten

Put the flour, salt, kalonji, sugar and yeast into a large bowl and mix well. Warm the milk until it is lukewarm, reserve 1 tbsp yogurt and add the rest to the milk and blend thoroughly. Melt the butter or ghee. Add the milk and yogurt mixture, egg and ghee or butter to the flour, knead with your hands or in a food processor until a soft and springy dough is formed. Place the dough in a large plastic food bag and tie up the uppermost part so that the dough has enough room for expansion. Rinse a bowl (preferably steel, as this will retain heat better) with hot water and put the bag of dough in it. Put the bowl in a warm place for ½-1 hour, until risen to double the original quantity.

Divide the dough into 8 balls, cover them and keep aside for 10-15 minutes. Preheat oven to 230°C/450°F/Gas Mark 8. Put an ungreased baking sheet into the oven to preheat for about 10 minutes. Remove baking sheet from the oven and line with a sheet of greased greaseproof paper or baking parchment.

Take one of the balls and stretch it gently with both hands to make a teardrop shape. Lay this on the baking sheet and press it gently to stretch it to about 15-20cm/6-7 inches in length, maintaining the teardrop shape at all times. Make 2-3 similar shapes at a time and brush with the reserved yogurt, then sprinkle with the sesame or poppy seeds. Bake on the top rung of the oven for 10-12 minutes, or until puffed and browned. Serve with any meat, chicken or vegetable curry.

Spiced Fruit Salad

Preparation Time: 10-15 minutes, plus 1 hour chilling time
Cooking Time: 20 minutes **Serves:** 6-8

A novel deviation from traditional Indian desserts, but an excellent one to round off an Indian meal. Handle the tinned mango slices very carefully as they tend to be far too soft. Use fresh mangoes instead if you have a friendly bank manager!

Ingredients

1 x 425g/15oz can pineapple chunks
1 x 425g/15oz can papaya (paw paw) chunks
1 x 425g/15oz can mango slices, cut into chunks
1 x 425g/15oz can guava halves, cut into chunks
3 × 5cm/2-inch cinnamon sticks
3 black cardamoms
6 whole cloves
8 black peppercorns

Drain all the fruits and reserve the syrup. Mix all the syrup together, reserve 570ml/1 pint and drain off remainder. Put the syrup into a saucepan and add the spices, bring to the boil, cover the pan and let it simmer for 20 minutes.

Uncover and reduce the syrup to half its original volume by boiling for 5-6 minutes. Remove from heat, cover, and allow the syrup to cool. (In an open pan some of the flavour will be lost.)

Reserve a few pieces of papaya and guava and all the mangoes. Arrange the remaining fruits in a serving bowl. Arrange the mangoes on top, then put in the reserved papaya and guava. Strain the spiced syrup and pour over the fruits. Cover with cling film and chill before serving.

Vermicelli Kheer

Preparation Time: 10 minutes **Cooking Time:** 20-25 minutes **Serves:** 6-8

In this popular pudding, the vermicelli is first lightly fried in ghee, then simmered gently in milk with sugar and spices to make a rich and creamy dish.

Ingredients

2 tbsps ghee or unsalted butter
30g/1oz plain vermicelli
30g/1oz sultanas
30g/1oz almonds, blanched and slivered
570ml/1 pint full cream milk
60g/2oz sugar
1 tbsp ground almonds
½ tsp ground cardamon
½ tsp ground cinnamon
1 tbsp rosewater or 5-6 drops of other flavourings such as vanilla or almond

Melt the ghee or butter over low heat and add the vermicelli, sultanas and slivered almonds. Stir and fry for 2-3 minutes until the vermicelli is golden brown. Add the milk, sugar and ground almonds, bring to the boil and simmer gently for 20 minutes, stirring frequently.

Stir in ground cardamom and cinnamon and remove the pan from heat. Allow the kheer to cool slightly and stir in the rosewater or other flavouring. Serve hot or cold.

Kulfi (Indian Ice Cream)

Preparation Time: 10 minutes **Cooking Time:** 15-20 minutes, plus 4-5 hours freezing time and 1½-1¾ hours softening time **Serves:** 6-8

Kulfi is by far the most popular ice cream in India. It is firmer than conventional ice cream and is usually set in small tin or aluminium moulds. You can, however, use either small yogurt pots or a plastic ice cream box.

Ingredients

150ml/5 fl oz fresh milk
2 tbsps ground rice
1 tbsp ground almonds
1 x 425g/15oz can evaporated milk
1 tsp ground cardamom
60g/2oz sugar
430ml/¾ pint double cream
1 tbsp rosewater or 5-6 drops of any other flavouring such as vanilla, almond etc.
30g/1oz shelled, unsalted pistachio nuts, lightly crushed

Heat the milk until it is lukewarm. Put the ground rice and ground almonds into a small bowl and gradually add the warm milk, a little at a time, and make a thin paste of pouring consistency. Stir continuously and break up any lumps, if any lumps remain, sieve the paste.

Heat evaporated milk to boiling point and add the ground cardamom. Take the pan off the heat and gradually add the almond/rice mixture, stirring continuously. Add the sugar and cream and place the pan over medium heat, cook the mixture for 12-15 minutes, stirring continuously. Remove the pan from heat and allow the mixture to cool slightly.

Add the rosewater and half the pistachio nuts, stir and mix well. Allow the mixture to cool completely, stirring frequently to prevent a skin from forming on the surface. When the mixture has cooled completely, put it into a plastic ice cream box or individual moulds. Top with the remaining pistachio nuts and place in the freezer or in the ice-making compartment of a refrigerator for 4-5 hours.

Remove the kulfi to the refrigerator for 1½-1¾ hours before serving. This will soften it slightly and will make it easier to cut into desired size when it is set in an ice cream box. The time required to soften the kulfi will vary according to the size of the container used.

Appetisers:
- Chicken Tikka 16
- Masala Machchi 10
- Onion Bhajiyas 14
- Seekh Kababs 12

Breads:
- Chapatties 54
- Naan 62

Cakes and Desserts:
- Kulfi (Indian Ice Cream) 68
- Spiced Fruit Salad 64
- Vermicelli Kheer 66

Chapatties 54
Chicken Chaat 18
Chicken Tikka 16
Chicken with Whole Spices 42
Coriander Chicken 30
Cucumber and Onion Raita 56
Egg and Potato Dum 24

Fish and Seafood:
- Fish Bhoona 28
- Prawn Chilli Masala 34

Fish Bhoona 28
Kheema Shahzada 20
Kofta Bhoona 36
Kulfi (Indian Ice Cream) 68
Masala Machchi 10
Meat Dilpasand 40

Meat Dishes:
- Kheema Shahzada 20
- Kofta Bhoona 36
- Meat Dilpasand 40
- Meat Madras 22
- Meat Samosas 48
- Meat Vindaloo 26
- Pasanda Badam Curry 32
- Rogan Josh 44
- Shahi Korma 46

Meat Madras 22
Meat Samosas 48
Meat Vindaloo 26
Mixed Vegetable Curry 38
Mushroom Bhaji 58
Naan 62
Onion Bhajiyas 14
Pasanda Badam Curry 32
Pilau Rice 50
Potatoes with Garlic and Chillies 60

Poultry:
- Chicken Chaat 18
- Chicken Tikka 16
- Chicken with Whole Spices 42
- Coriander Chicken 30

Prawn Chilli Masala 34
Rogan Josh 44
Saag Bhaji 52
Seekh Kababs 12
Shahi Korma 46
Spiced Fruit Salad 64

Side Dishes:
- Cucumber and Onion Raita 56
- Egg and Potato Dum 24
- Mushroom Bhaji 58
- Pilau Rice 50
- Potatoes with Garlic and Chillies 60
- Saag Bhaji 52

Vermicelli Kheer 66